DISCOVERING
COGGESHALL

For Alan Willis, who organized the funding and
launched the Discovering Coggeshall project

DISCOVERING COGGESHALL

Timber-framed buildings in the town centre

David Stenning with Richard Shackle

I am sensible, that the want of this Caution is the Foundation of that great Misfortune we have in matters of ancient History; in which the Impudence, the Ribaldry, the empty Flourishes, the little Regard to Truth, and the Fondness of telling a strange Story, has dwindled a great many valuable Pieces of ancient History into meer Romance.

Daniel Defoe 1704

Published by
John Lewis of Coggeshall, England

www.discoveringcoggeshall.co.uk

© Coggeshall Heritage Society

ISBN 978-0-9539165-1-1

CONTENTS

FOREWORD

The country towns of Essex can astonish those who are not familiar with them. Little touched in many instances by the spread of London and busy roads, their centres have remained elegant and full of fine buildings. Coggeshall is a perfect example. Built on the River Blackwater as the adjunct of a Cistertian abbey and developed by clothiers, it has held its shape and retained much of its original meaning. Along with Braintree and other nearby communities it became lively with puritan argument in the 17th century but has since, like Maldon, held onto its residential pattern of timber building and the quietness which they establish. Essex was a great forest and its people lived in forest clearings with unlimited timber at their disposal. Wood provided everything they needed, from warmth, shelter and trade, to great art. Coggeshall's wooden streets offer everything from ancient workshops and humble dwellings to the great oaken 'palace' of Paycockes. The Heritage Society's gazetteer is a very special architectural guide. It lets one into the secret of Essex - why its trees more than any other native asset have created the soul of this beautiful county.

Ronald Blythe

PREFACE

Today, Coggeshall is regarded as a village. In the past, it was a significant town. Tied largely to clothmaking, its location and circumstances discouraged further expansion and it suffered progressive decline. As a result, it retains much of the fabric of the late medieval and Tudor town, the commercial areas and buildings now transformed to residential use. These two functions were always intermingled, so the change has taken place easily without much loss of old buildings or historic fabric.

To present day eyes, Coggeshall does not look like a town, lacking well defined retail or municipal areas or industrial activity. There are few large modern buildings, and few which have had their ground floors disfigured by large glazed shopfronts. Church Street, now a peaceful residential street, was the major highway and denoted 'The High Street' in the 1841 census. Trades like brewing and lacemaking have left little trace.

The buildings have been updated, with pitched roofs parallel to the street with hipped ends replacing gables, and with new facades with regularly spaced sash windows expressive of 18th and 19th century gentility. Late medieval Coggeshall, as can be seen from the reconstructions, was orderly and surprisingly uniform. Far from notions of picturesque disorder, utility and harmony would have been the overall impression. House and general building form would have been determined by the carpenters, and the particularities of the individual plot. The structural bays into which the timber frames divide impose a discipline which would determine room sizes, only partially affected by the owner's requirements. The degree of embellishment, now difficult to determine, was more the responsibility of the owner and gave scope for him to demonstrate wealth and status.

Surveying Coggeshall for this gazetteer has been an enormous task. Buildings in occupation are difficult to measure, plastered walls and domestic and commercial fittings all being obstacles. Many buildings have been sub-divided, making access complicated and it difficult to see them as a whole. Such surveys can rarely be more than partial, with some parts remaining unexplored.

In contrast, a building such as the former Cricketers public house, undergoing renovation, will prove very rewarding. What would otherwise require guesswork to fill in the detail can be viewed at a glance and a complete record achieved. The patience of owners has been essential to the success of this exercise, and invariably the good people of Coggeshall proved hospitable and accommodating. We wish to say thank you for the splendid welcomes, the excellent conversation and endless cups of coffee.

ACKNOWLEDGEMENTS

This small book, and the work of the Discovering Coggeshall project that is continuing on buildings in the centre of the town, could not have been undertaken without financial and other commitments from many people.

The greatest contribution has been from those house owners and tenants of Coggeshall who allowed their homes and shops to be invaded, drawn, photographed and measured, some of them several times. We must thank all those people for their tolerance and good humour. Their contribution to the nation's permanent records of timber-framed buildings is analogous to those who contribute a treasured family document to a library.

The originating financial contribution was a legacy from Stanley Prentice, for many years the chemist of the town, but the Coggeshall Heritage Society, by donation and by guarantees from members, built up sufficient funds to justify application to the Heritage Lottery Fund, whose generous grant created the bulk of the core funding.

We are grateful to other donors especially Coggeshall Parish Council, the Council for British Archaeology, the Essex Environment Trust, the Essex Heritage Trust, the Essex Historic Buildings Group and the Vernacular Architecture Group.

Many others have given of their time and resources and we thank them all. We owe an especial debt to the other members of the Discovering Coggeshall survey team who have contributed their knowledge of the buildings in the town, particularly John Walker and Brenda Watkin and Elphin Watkin, and those who have helped edit and put this book together, namely David Andrews, Michael Bowes, Keith Cullum and John Lewis.

All our donors have been supportive during difficult periods and we are grateful for that as for the financial support.

INTRODUCTION

The layout and plan of the medieval house

The plan of a house reflects the way its inhabitants lived. Research has identified a standard medieval plan form, against which a surviving building can be compared. This plan form is hierarchical inasmuch as there is a central hall, either side of which is a high end and a more utilitarian low end.

This is a particularly English phenomenon, and is seldom found in Europe. The hall was open to the roof and had a central hearth. It was a communal space where the household dined and conducted its daily business. The hall was entered through opposed front and rear doors leading into a cross-passage, from which doors led into the low end, which generally contained two rooms, the buttery and pantry. These were for food and drink, but in suitable locations the one abutting the street may serve as a shop (as in the illustration). At the high end, there is a room interpreted as a parlour providing private accommodation for the owner. Over the two ends, there were usually upstairs chambers, the largest of which is sometimes called the solar. There were often further structures, such as a kitchen, behind or at one end of the house.

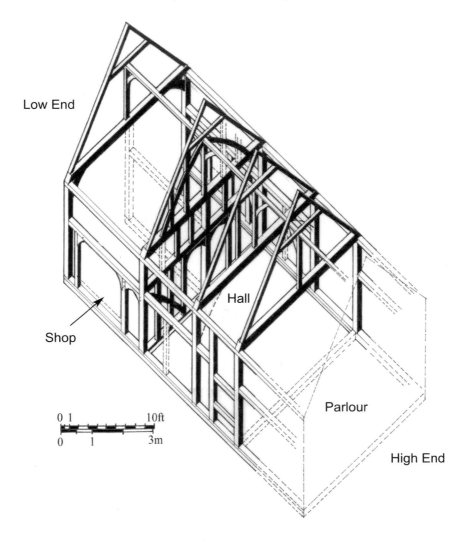

Low End

Hall

Shop

0 1   10ft
0   1   3m

Parlour

High End

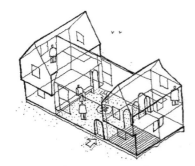

H-plan with two cross-wings

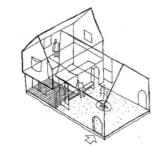

L-plan with a single end

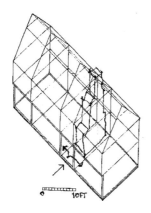

Lobby-entry plan

As time went by, the high and low ends, with their small upper chambers, partly in the roof space, were considered inadequate. They were therefore often rebuilt, in the form of jettied (projecting at the front) cross-wings, either one forming an L-shaped plan, or two giving an H-plan. The general plan form in these enlarged houses remained the same. Where there are two cross-wings, they are rarely of the same date, showing that the improvements took place over a period of time.

From the mid 15th century, chimney stacks began to be constructed, often on the rear wall of the hall. This allowed the entire building to have an upper floor throughout, with a jetty running the full length of the front wall, producing the so-called 'long wall jetty' house. This created a large chamber over the hall, which could be used in a variety of ways which are rarely clear today. Fully floored buildings had probably occurred even earlier in dense urban areas where space was at a premium.

Chimney stacks could be provided in a number of different locations as these new features were assimilated into the design of the house. In Essex, it typically backed on to the cross-passage where it helped define this as a corridor. In Suffolk, it is more commonly found at the high end of the hall. Separate chimneys might also be provided for the parlour and other parts of the house.

The introduction of the chimney stack led to a new plan form, the baffle- or lobby-entry plan, in which the front door leads into a lobby formed by the side of the stack, and there is usually a staircase on the other side of the stack. Initially the chimney was placed off-centre in the house, but later it came to occupy a central position, making it possible for the façade to be designed symmetrically around a central front door. Lobby-entry houses were built from early in the 17th century and became very widespread in England, and indeed migrated to North America with the first settlers.

In towns and cities, the density of settlement led to different types of plan form where buildings were typically disposed with their narrow ends to the street. This however is often not the case in the small market towns of Essex, for reasons that have yet to be fully explained.

In the early days of a town like Coggeshall, the available space was divided up into regular plots, often called burgage plots, though technically burgage refers to a type of relatively free tenure. Frontage space, particularly in central locations, was valuable and these plots came to be subdivided. The resulting narrower units meant that there was less space for the standard tripartite parlour/hall/services plan, and inevitably the buildings tended to expand into the depth of the plots. This process is little understood, and it is hoped that this project in Coggeshall will shed some light on it.

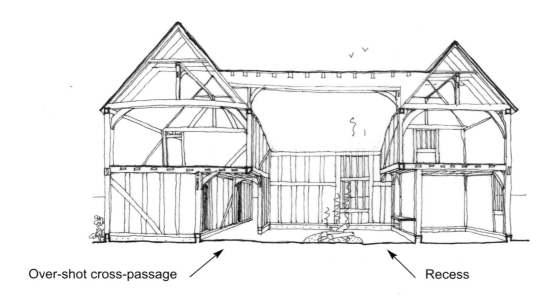

Over-shot cross-passage   Recess

Narrowing plot widths prompted inventive house planning and on occasions the cross-passage was relocated under the flank of the adjoining cross-wing or upper chamber. This was common in Coggeshall and is usually described as an over-shot cross-passage. Similarly the owner's bench at the high end of the hall is sometimes found under a recess formed below the upper floor of the parlour.

House types in Coggeshall

The basic house typology, as discussed above, can be discerned in the surviving buildings of Coggeshall. However, there is the usual problem arising from the low survival rate of the medieval open hall. Halls are rare, whereas cross-wings abound because at two full storeys they were readily adaptable and could, with minor modifications, continue in use.

The halls that have survived are those that were tall enough to function with a later inserted floor (e.g. Baumanns Restaurant, Chapel Inn, White Hart, Through Inn). On occasions the height and length of a former open hall can be determined by a few significant clues (e.g. 18 Stoneham Street).

Where buildings, usually cross-wings were of three original storeys, the upper floor has usually been removed. The three storey cross-wing at the White Hart (now Cavendish House) is a rare exception. More surprisingly, the rear bays of cross-wings have often been removed making their original length difficult to determine. This is all about patterns of adaptation, with continued usefulness the key factor.

Only one aisled hall survives in a readily recognisable form (The Bull, 47 Church Street) and that only in a schematic sense. It is probable that a great deal of it does survive, but invisible beneath later finishes and claddings.

It is suggested that there were formerly a number of aisled halls in Coggeshall. We come to this conclusion by following clues as to the disposition of structures, in the way that 'shadows' are still present after their removal. The arrangement of bracing in flank walls is another possible clue, as this tended to follow a symmetrical pattern about the centre line of the hall. Most of our proposals are of the single rear aisle form, where this aisle would have been invisible from the street (e.g. 12 East Street). The potential size of the hall is another pertinent factor as some would seem improbably small without the addition of an aisle.

3

Without firm evidence, in the form of structural remains or clear identifiable mortice holes, these views must remain purely speculative. The rear aisle at 7 Market End seems somewhat more defensible. This arrangement, with the service doors sited to the rear, has been detected in other locations. A public house in Churchgate Street, Old Harlow, has its rear aisle surviving complete.

Aisles probably continued to be provided later than is usually found, as a response to limited urban frontage widths. With these aisles, the halls could gain in useful space despite the limitations of a narrow plot.

It seems likely that from the 12th to the 14th centuries Coggeshall consisted largely of houses of the in-line type. Some recognisably survive, such as the impressively large Spooners (30 Church Street). Some would have been single ended (75-77 Church Street) and others, no doubt arranged in speculative groups built for renting out. It is probable that many remnants of the in-line form also exist, now submerged under later stages of improvement (Through Inn, 17-19 East Street). Such up-dating of more basic accommodation can leave relatively little evidence. Where a cross-wing is exceptionally narrow (18 East Street, 57 Stoneham Street) it would seem sensible to suggest that this was determined by a previous in-line end. A more complete understanding of this problem would require a more intrusive examination of all the remaining buildings.

Completely stripped timber frames in the nearby towns of Colchester and Maldon, have permitted a greater understanding of this process of gradual improvement. Houses with cross-wings of relatively broad frontage width would probably not have been so constrained and so would not have been single ended.

The large number of cross-wings with undershot cross-passages was not unexpected, though they proved even more common than anticipated. Usually, the standard house plan is modified in that the solar, or best upper room, is placed over this cross-wing. Whilst the solar is then at the low end, it benefits from the greater frontage width of these cross-wings.

These low end cross-wings, which include the cross-passage, can be of two or three bays in depth. Sometimes there is a separate single bay room on the ground floor (often a shop when it is at the front) and there may be a single bay room on the first. Sometimes, the latter will be a chamber over the shop (29 East Street). Single rear bays, on the ground floor are less easy to label.

High end cross-wings are noticeably rarer and found where there is a full H-plan dwelling. Where there are two cross-wings they appear to be of different dates, suggesting a slow process of evolution. A surprising number of high-ends have a bench recess and one even appears in the in-line Spooners. Whilst this device helps to reduce the frontage width, it also had had intrinsic merits in enhancing the visual impact of the bench location. The beam over the recess can be moulded, but our examples are not as elaborate as Kentish examples.

With these cross-wings, it is often impossible to determine the original position of the stairs. It is probable that a great variety of location was a feature of Coggeshall houses, including rising from the hall to a door in the flank.

The solar, wherever located, can be surprisingly large and this may represent an element of storage use. Comparing room sizes is instructive. The solar will usually be the largest upper room whether it is at the high or low end of a hall. Obviously there is a problem as the precise function of any of these upper rooms could change over time. The solar at The Chapel Inn (312 sq. ft.) is of a size compatible with what is a substantial mansion. Baumanns Restaurant seems to be a full H-plan house and its even larger solar (the exact dimensions difficult to define) again suits its pretentions. Solars with open-halls vary between 250 to 300 sq. ft., which seems disproportionally large in respect of the other accommodation. By this reckoning the room over the parlour at 7 Church Street (210 sq. ft.) seems to be too small for a solar and there is likely to have been a now missing element, elsewhere on the site.

The purpose built early 16th century solar at Paycockes is, at 185 sq. ft., remarkably small and must suggest a difference of function. There was, of course, a pre-existing solar, belonging to the earlier building. The late 16th century long-wall jetty houses must have solars that reflect changed functions and big new solars will have been markedly different in purpose.

The next stage in the course of house development is the appearance of the long-wall jetty house. There are relatively few of these surviving as early purpose built units and 7-9 West Street is a good example. More numerous are two bay 15th century long-wall jetty buildings where the use of the various rooms can be difficult to decide. They sometimes have two unequal bays and it is tempting to believe that the narrow bay held a shop (24 Church Street).

The relative lack of purpose built 15th to early 16th century long-wall jetty houses probably represents a dip in building activity. However, during this period, a number of the taller formerly open-hall houses were modified, to appear as long-wall jetties. In other cases the hall was demolished, and a jettied two storey unit with hall and chamber over, was inserted in its place. Where open halls were so modified the process could be disruptive obscuring evidence for the exact nature of the original structures.

By the mid 16th century, the purpose built long-wall jetty was being built in some numbers, often taking the place of an earlier structure.

Houses from the mid 16th century are sometimes referred to as 'transitional'. There exist a variety of plan forms that suggest an experimental approach to their layout and a lack of a clear view as to a desirable outcome. Some buildings, such as The Fleece public house, retain the old in-line plan arrangement, with a cross-passage in the expected, low end position. The Fleece was built in the early 17th century, with the chimney stacks on the rear wall in a pragmatic but un-integrated fashion. The provision of rear wall stacks for long-wall jetty houses seems a fairly early solution, and in some cases (51, 53, 55 Church Street) they were later re-built in axial positions inside the house. House plans such as 25 Church Street are difficult to explain: the location of the front door remains unknown. The cross-passage, as a simple straight through feature, seems gradually to have lost favour and front and rear corridor-like doors came eventually to be offset.

Nationally, the lobby-entry (or baffle entry) plan type began to become popular probably from the 1580s. Here the stack was axially placed, in its own framing bay, with fireplaces to hall and parlour. This system allowed an entrance lobby against the front of the stack and sometimes room for a staircase behind it. Such plans can indicate slight changes in room function, variable in different areas of Britain, but with the hall losing some of its status. In some instances, the parlour ought perhaps to be labelled a 'kitchen' as it becomes less clear where cooking was taking place. Traditional service rooms tend to become more difficult to identify and may be relegated to auxiliary structures to the rear. This plan type seems often to be found with a staircase-tower to the rear but 12 Church Street seems the only example in Coggeshall.

The Old Oak, Stoneham Street and Hutleys, 57 Church Street, both 17th century, are classic baffle-entry houses. Curiously, neither had a structural partition between their two-bay halls and the supposed end service bay. With The Old Oak there is now a somewhat later partition to provide a present-day kitchen.

Paycockes House, nationally famous, is a long-wall jetty house of the early 16th century. Its plan form is extremely peculiar and its interpretation the subject of ongoing debate. The provision of a part third storey with attic storage is somewhat precocious and this feature was copied, in the 17th century, by the builder of the adjoining Fleece public house.

The oddness of Paycockes was clearly motivated by the need to incorporate a pre-existing house. This, the third best house of John Paycocke, father of the Thomas who built the existing house in 1509, was mostly to the rear of today's building and may have substantially survived as ancillary accommodation.

Much of the changes to the houses, over time, were prompted by the need for more privacy and larger private spaces. The parlour and the solar were most involved and a new solar/parlour block, to the rear was sometimes provided. Paycockes and Spooners are examples.

Purpose built kitchens either attached or detached were always a useful adjunct. Very few have been identified. Probable kitchens have been recognised at The Chapel Inn, 19 East Street and 61 Stoneham Street, but there are likely to have been many more. Some of the extended rear wings may have served such a function but the evidence is rarely conclusive.

Houses apparently of two unequal bays are a puzzling feature of many urban centres which have given rise to much debate. Where information about the original elevation design, or internal planning, is thin, the type is difficult to explain.

Shops and houses

The majority of surviving shops occur as part of a recognisable house. They can be combined with all the usually encountered house types and frequently take the place of a service room. Coggeshall clearly had numerous shops throughout the town, and they are typical in size and detail with those elsewhere. The shop that forms part of The Woolpack public house (91 Church Street) is one of the best preserved examples in England.

1 Church Street, is a remarkable example of a pair of near identical shops with solars above them. These appear frequently in the literature, but rarely survive to be recognised. The question arises as to the use of these little solars. It is probable that they were basic living accommodation and may have been heated by charcoal braziers. Alternatively, they may simply be for storage, perhaps with an apprentice living in.

40 Church Street (Craig Dhu) is one of at least a pair of very small single-ended houses, with a shop in the cross-wing. Such houses, likely to have been built speculatively for renting out, are more often found in the 'Wealden' format as has been recognised at 22 Church Street. It took little to evolve a long-wall jetty version where there is a chamber over the hall.

Shops can vary in size from as small as 30 sq. ft. to as much as 200. Most often, they are between 80 and 100 sq. ft. and the Coggeshall examples are of this range. They comprise a small squarish room with a shop window to the street. These are either of 'half-arch' form or a series of four centred arches. The two types seem alternatives, rather than a significant indicator of use. Sometimes there is a door to the frontage, occasionally of narrow coffin door type (e.g. The Woolpack, 91 Church Street), but more often access is gained indirectly from a door in the flank of the cross-passage. Most Coggeshall examples seem to be of the 'half-arch' type (e.g. Through Inn, 17-19 East Street), but there seems to have been a 'full arch' at 4 West Street.

Market Stalls

These could vary from a boot-fair-like table to a completely permanent structure. Over the years they tended to become more elaborate until they became dwellings, often still with a shop. The market area at Market End and West Street retains 'booth stalls', that were permanent but lacked a domestic use. That at 10 Market End is a remarkable survivor, with its cross-passage, double jettying and a loft over. The other stalls survive less complete, but exhibit the characteristics of the 'row' buildings which were typical of market infill. It is clear that West Street was once much wider, but obstructed by these lines of buildings.

Carpentry technique

The buildings of Coggeshall belong predictably to the north Essex vernacular tradition. Nevertheless, there is more variety than one would expect, suggesting that the carpenters had often come from surrounding towns.

Main posts often do not have jowls as is commonplace in the wider Colchester environs. However early ones do have jowls, such as Spooners (30 Church Street). Jowls become normal practice from the mid 16th century and tend to have the long attenuated profiles normal into the 17th century.

Wall bracing is invariably of the tension type with down braces, but braces are relatively few, and usually stop at a stud in the 'Colchester carpentry' fashion. A good exception is Paycocke's House where the pattern probably has a structural function and is consistent throughout the structure. The ogee brace in Spooners is a rare example of East Anglian decorative tradition of the 14th century. The serpentine braces at 3 Albert Place and 51-53 Church Street belong to a national fashion beginning to be felt from the mid 16th century. The mid-rails in nos. 1 and 2 Market Hill are part of the same exotic tradition that perhaps owes its origins to the Midlands.

Normally Essex bracing is on the outside of a wall until the 16th century when it tends to move inside. In Coggeshall, there are a number instance of internal braces occurring at an earlier date, where they were intended to decorate a room interior.

The floor joist joint with soffit tenons and diminished haunches was, in Essex, usually taken up in the early 16th century. In contrast, Coggeshall floor joists seem to retain the plain soffit tenons, well into that century. The splayed joint, with central tenon is often thought to be rare but can be found in the former 'Cricketers' and in no. 61 Stoneham Street.

Primary bracing, in which the braces are inserted first and the studs fitted to them, usually straight and sometimes upwardly inclined (e.g. The Fleece, West Street) can be seen from the late 16th century.

In Essex we expect crown-post roofs up until the mid 16th century. Simple longitudinal braces, to the collar purlin, are usual. These gradually reduce in width, until they became so thin as to be nominal by the time that this type of roof went out of fashion.

The Bull at 47 Church Street is the only example of the 'uniform scantling' typical of the early or archaic carpentry style. However, the reused rafters of Spooners probably belonged to the same tradition.

There are a number of octagonal crown-posts, with moulded capitals, all a feature of higher status buildings (e.g. Chapel Inn, Baumanns Restaurant). Crown-posts on 'open' trusses with tension or down braces, usually a feature of north west Essex, predominate.

The Chapel Inn has splayed scarf joints with under squinted abutments, typical of the 14th century. The wall bracing is of the fan pattern also typical of East Anglia at this time.

The queen post carpentry of the White Hart Hotel points to a south Suffolk source. There are a small number of such roofs scattered just south of the Essex/Suffolk border. Clasped side purlin roofs are the common choice after the the crown-post went out of fashion. Earlier examples can have a single tier of wind braces. Their omission can help determine the pre-existence of a stack bay. Butt purlin roofs have proved to be rare in the town, but 16 East Street is an example that eased the provision of dormers. 1 Albert Place is an earlier mid 16th century example. One house in Church Street has a hollowed out bell capital on the external post, belonging to a Suffolk tradition.

There are three buildings where a central post appears in a cross-wing rear wall (18 Stoneham Street). The purpose of such a post, which seems unnecessary, remains unknown. Similarly mysterious are the single grooves on the soffit of a bressumer, presumably to house shutters.

Hearths and heating

The earlier houses would have been heated by a hearth in the open hall which may also have been utilised for cooking. Generally the smoke would have exited via the roof, although Coggeshall seems to have few of the gablets to let the smoke out that are otherwise common in Essex. The evidence consists of sooted roof timbers which can occasionally be seen in the town. The White Hart and Chapel Inn each retain remnants of octagonal smoke louvres, though their external appearance is uncertain. The little industrial building behind 6 East Street must have had something similar, but more utilitarian.

It is probable that braziers were also used, particularly in upper rooms. The gablets in the roof of The Cricketers could have been for the exit of smoke from the first floor room.

When examining timber buildings it is not unusual to find evidence for chimney stacks which pre-date the use of brick. Many buildings have a hole in the rear or the flank of a timber frame to contain such a chimney stack. Sometimes this has been replaced by a 16th century brick stack closely adjoining the same location. Presumably these stacks were structurally weak and do not survive.

However we have two 'primitive' stack openings in Coggeshall. 18 Stoneham Street has a framed gap in the flank opening to the parlour and cellar. It has a pair of empty mortices, towards the solar, near the top of the opening. It also has two similar mortices near the base. A similar arrangement can be seen in 18 East Street, again within the parlour and solar. In this case the girt is interrupted and there is a timber fixed across the gap, on the outside, just beneath the top plate. Here the first floor structure is complicated and has been strengthened, probably to support a first floor hearth. How such stacks functioned remains unknown. In Paycocke's House there are a pair of 'fireplace gaps', one on each floor of the partition between the hall and service rooms. Curiously there is absolutely no provision for the exiting of smoke. Perhaps they were intended to contain charcoal braziers, but were soon supplanted by a conventional stack on the rear wall. A further theory is addressed in the relevant text.

The use of brick for chimney stacks was only slowly adopted. The first seem to appear in the early 15th century, but remained uncommon until the mid 16th century. Stone for stacks seems to have been unobtainable except at high social status. We are however fortunate that two early stacks survive in Coggeshall. These are made of alternate courses of clay roof tiles, bricks and cobbles, laid in a grainy mortar. Both the buildings, the Chapel Inn and 14 East Street are architecturally ambitious. Stone nevertheless was also used for decorative fireplace surrounds (mantel arch and jambs) in no. 6 and 14 East Street.

There are numerous chimney stacks, with timber mantel beams of the 16th and 17th centuries. These can be difficult to date, particularly as both bricks and mantel beams were commonly reused, a process still happening today. 15 East Street has a late 16th century 'nostril fireplace', with special air draught flues in the rear of the hearth. These are a curiosity, about seven of them have been found, mainly in central Essex. This is probably a late example, the internally curved hearth and small neat bricks suggesting a late 16th century date.

'Nostril' fireplace, 15 East Street

The Gazetteer

The gazetteer contains street by street descriptions of all the timber-framed buildings surveyed in Coggeshall. These are homes, full of furniture and belongings, and so much of the structure will be concealed. The drawings are an attempt to illustrate the visible fabric with the minimum of interpretation. The temptation to speculate to complete the picture has been resisted.

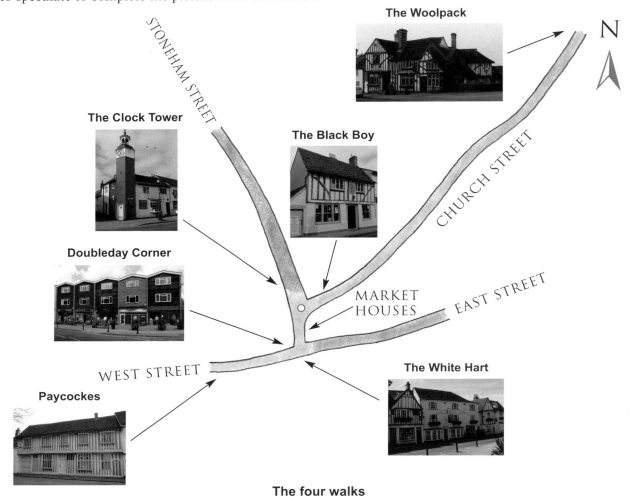

The four walks

All the listed walks start from the centre of the town. Church Street runs north-east on the north side towards the church and the Woolpack, returning on the south side. Similarily East Street runs eastwards on the north side (the left hand moving towards Colchester) and returning along the south side. The West Street walk goes out from the centre towards Paycockes and returns on the north side. Stoneham Street runs from the centre near the Chapel Inn and Clock Tower on the west side and returns on the east side. The Market Hill and Market End buildings follow an anti-clockwise route in the central crossroads, starting at Doubleday Corner, outside the Co-op.

Your exploration may be lengthy. Fortunately there are two good inns in this small area; Chapel Inn and the Woolpack. There is also the White Hart Hotel, the well-known restaurant Baumanns, and two good cafés, the Black Boy and the Clock Tower.

CHURCH STREET

The walk begins on the north side of Church Street and returns on the south side

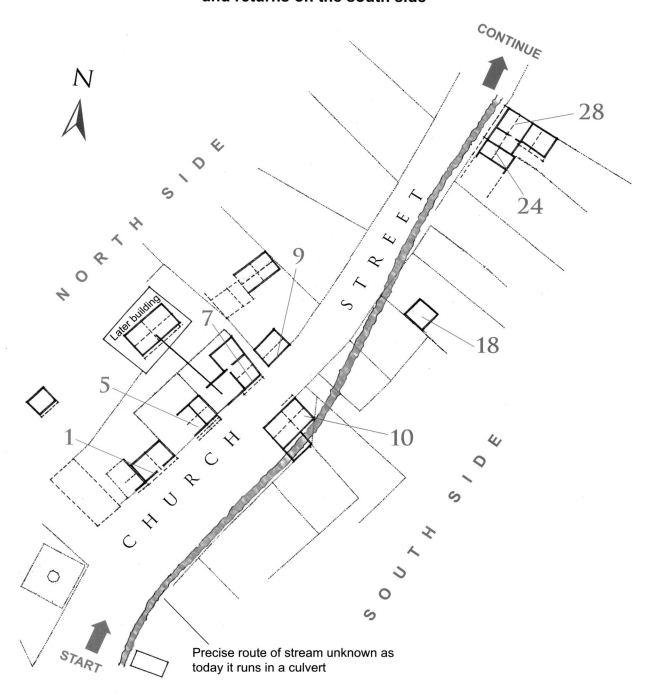

Precise route of stream unknown as today it runs in a culvert

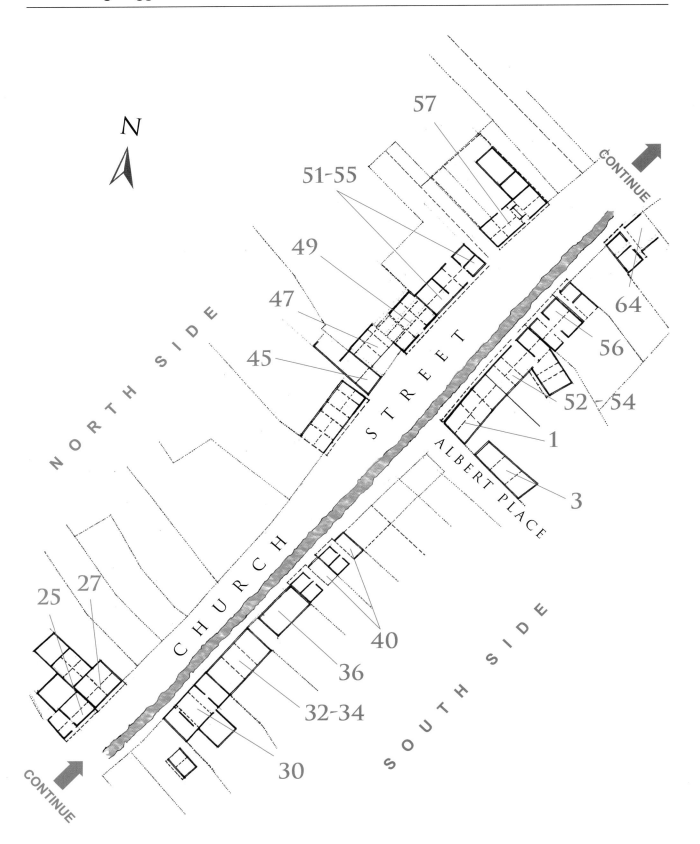

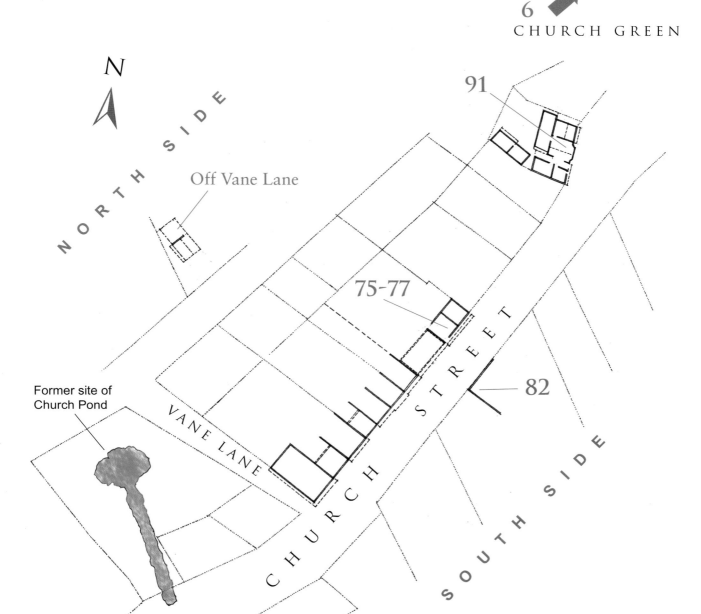

N

NORTH SIDE

6 CHURCH GREEN

91

Off Vane Lane

75-77

82

Former site of
Church Pond

VANE LANE

CHURCH STREET

SOUTH SIDE

CONTINUE

CHURCH STREET - NORTH SIDE

1 Church Street

A pair of virtually identical shops, with solars over. To the south-west there was an early cross-wing, of which only one wall survives. These shops must have been speculative development and it would be interesting to know whether the first-floor solars were domestic accommodation, or were intended for apprentices and storage. There were no fireplaces for heating, but brasiers could have been used.

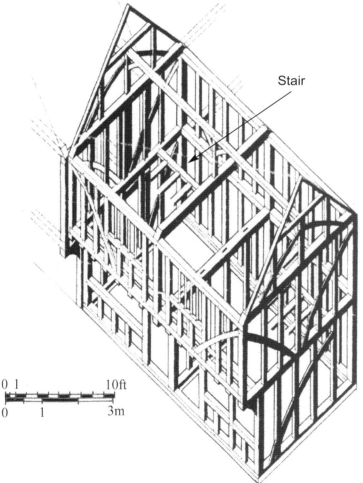

Stair

0 1   10ft

0   1   3m

The 'half-arch' shop fronts are identical except that the eastern unit has an additional central mullion. In general central mullions were used to enable the fitting of smaller, internal shutters.

5 Church Street

This is a two storey jettied structure of the 17th century of two unequal bays. The front elevation has a simple moulded jetty fascia and two wide symmetrically disposed windows on the first floor. To the west is one surviving wall of a three-storey jettied building. The 1575 rental survey suggests that this extended by at least a bay, to the east and west. A structure of three bays seems most likely, with its hall to the western side. The extent of the probable eastern bay is delineated by a dotted line on the drawing.

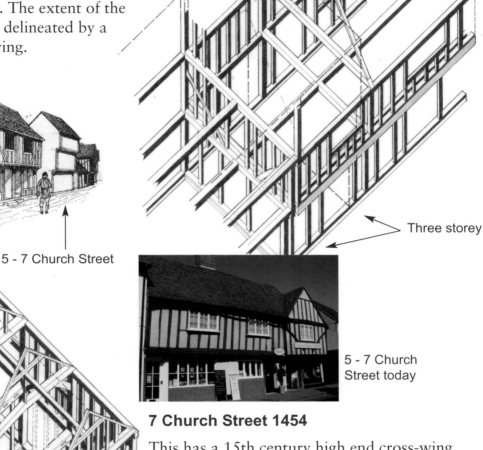

5 - 7 Church Street

Three storey

5 - 7 Church Street today

Hall

0 1   10ft

0   1   3m

7 Church Street 1454

This has a 15th century high end cross-wing with a two-bay room over the parlour, and a bench recess facing into the hall. This was one of the first high end recesses to be identified in Essex, and we now know that they were a popular feature in Coggeshall. The room functions in the rear bay remain unclear. In comparison with other buildings, the upper front room seems too small to be a solar and a further cross-wing, now demolished, at the other end seems likely.

9 Church Street

This is a cross-wing like structure that includes part of the rear wall of a 16th century long-wall jetty house, moved from elsewhere. There are traces of a late medieval building to the rear that is too ephemeral to measure.

25 Church Street

A long-wall jetty house with only a single end, it probably dates from the mid 16th century, and has an almost symmetrical front first floor elevation. The south-western bay may have had a form of cross-passage to the rear yard. The internal doors, one above the other, are perplexing. The much obscured rear wing may be contemporary and probably contained the services.

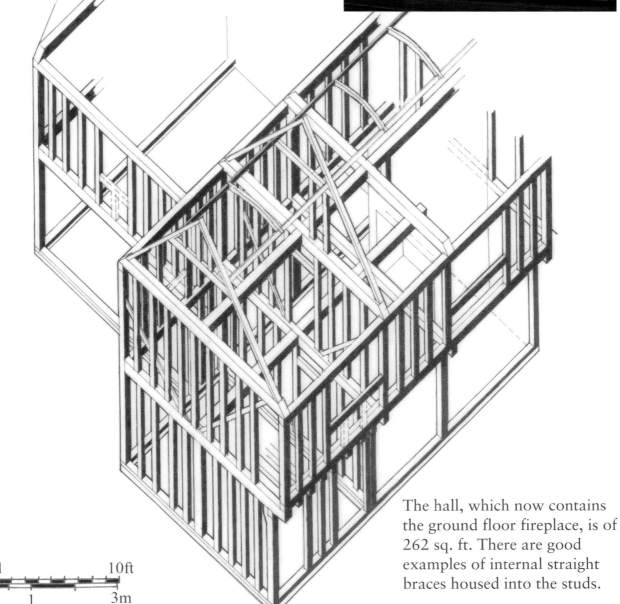

The hall, which now contains the ground floor fireplace, is of 262 sq. ft. There are good examples of internal straight braces housed into the studs.

0 1   10ft

0   1   3m

27 Church Street (Saunders)

A late 15th-century building of high quality carpentry and closely spaced studwork, it was probably originally three-storeyed. The two-bay plan means that it is unlikely to have originally been a house, and a public use is suggested. On the front elevation, a bell capital is cusped and hollowed in the Suffolk manner. The structure to the rear is likely to be earlier, and to have a specialised function related to the cloth trade. Its rear wall is angled, probably reflecting an earlier boundary.

Rear range woolhall?

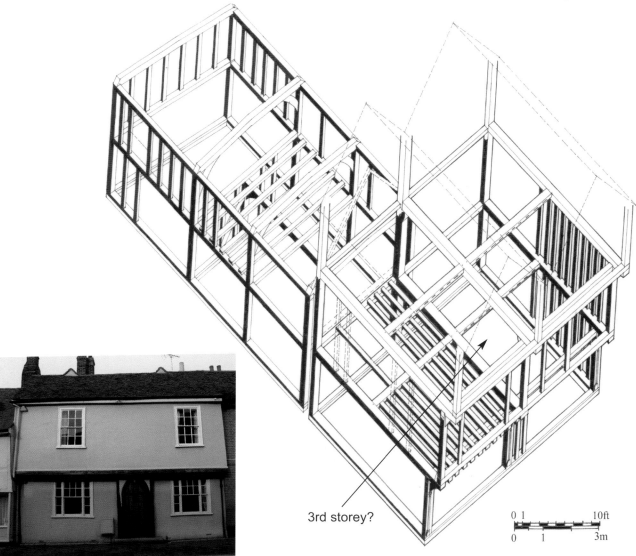

3rd storey?

45 Church Street

A late 16th century cross-wing with jowled posts, but with much of the fabric obscured. One open truss has solid braces, rising to a tie-beam or low collar. The roof is hipped, with a gablet to the rear. Behind this is a two-bay un-jettied structure of relatively early framing. It has a 'radiating' pattern of wall bracing and a window on the east face, ground floor. This very small building may have been a parlour/solar for the adjoining aisled hall to the east. This would assume that it has been moved a short distance onto the neighbouring plot.

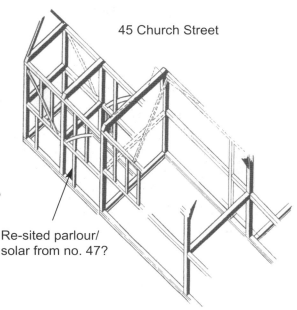

45 Church Street

Re-sited parlour/ solar from no. 47?

The Bull

47 Church Street (formerly The Bull)

This is probably early 14th century and the oldest secular building in Coggeshall. It is a single aisled and single-ended hall house. The 'end' was incorporated into no. 49 in the 16th century. It is probable that 47/49 were then in one ownership although the use of no. 49 remains in doubt. It is suggested that the little two-bay structure at no. 45 was once a parlour/solar extension to no. 47. The crown-post roof seems an original feature.

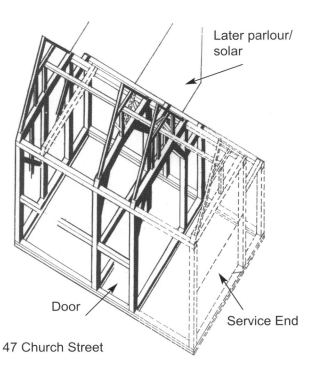

Later parlour/ solar

Door

Service End

47 Church Street

45 - 47 Church Street

19

49 Church Street

This mysterious building is now L-shaped, but originally incorporated the end of the adjoining aisled hall with the roof, or roofs, covering the completed square block. A pyramidal roof is possible but a double range of hips, as in the drawing, is more likely as the north flank was clearly hipped. Of the mid 16th century, it was certainly not a conventional dwelling, and probably had a commercial use. The front elevation had first floor oriel windows, arranged symmetrically, and a moulded and carved bressumer. This was clearly an expensive building with very closely spaced studwork and a large span. The peculiar arrangement of the floor joists is probably significant but eludes explanation.

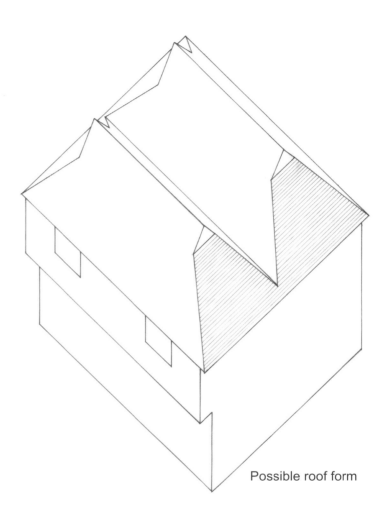

Possible roof form

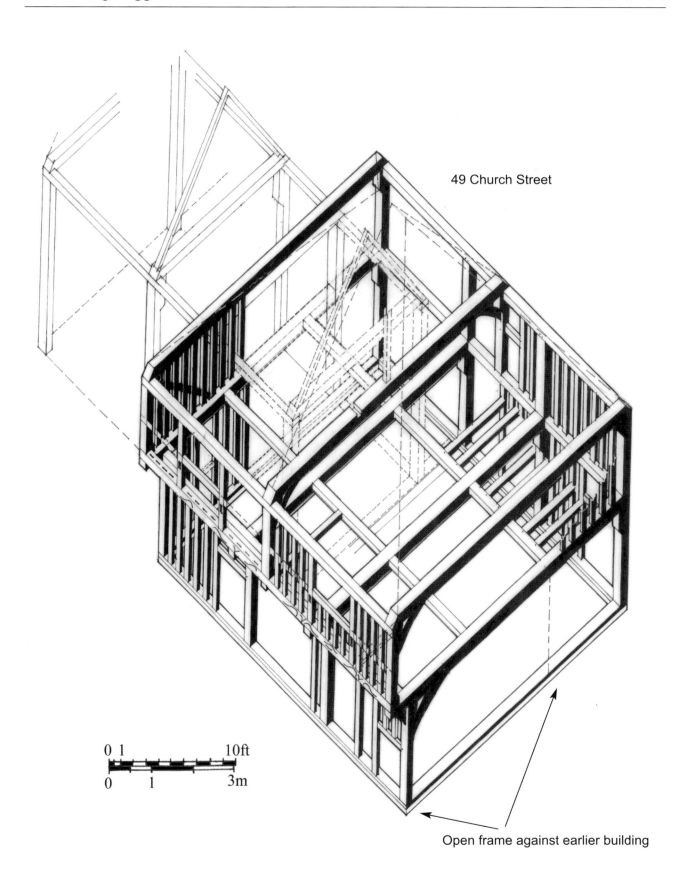

49 Church Street

0 1   10ft
0   1   3m

Open frame against earlier building

51 - 55 Church Street

This is a large but conventional long-wall jetty house of the late 16th century. It is curious that the carved jetty bressumer has two different merchant's marks. The three sections of the bressumer also have different patterns, and were clearly carved by different craftsmen. To further confuse matters, the differing merchant's marks appear on the same part. There is a flexibility of bay framing that is often found at the end of the 16th century. The parlour is surprisingly large. The ground-floor hall measures 310 sq. ft. It is likely that the original chimney stack was at the high end of the rear wall. Soon after, this was replaced with a central stack against the parlour wall. There also seems to have been a small fireplace in the back wall of the rear service room.

53 - 55 Church Street

The solar originally had a projecting oriel, probably supported on the grotesque corbels which later decorated a door hood. Part of the carved bressumer is remarkably similar to one in East Street dated 1585. The remarkable serpentine bracing in the upper front elevation, an occasional feature of Essex houses of this period, may well owe its origins to the Midlands. The roof originally carried on over to overlap the hipped roof of nos. 45 - 47.

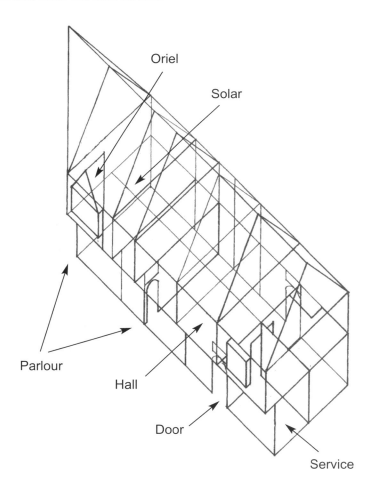

Oriel

Solar

Parlour

Hall

Door

Service

A section of the bressumer showing a merchant's mark

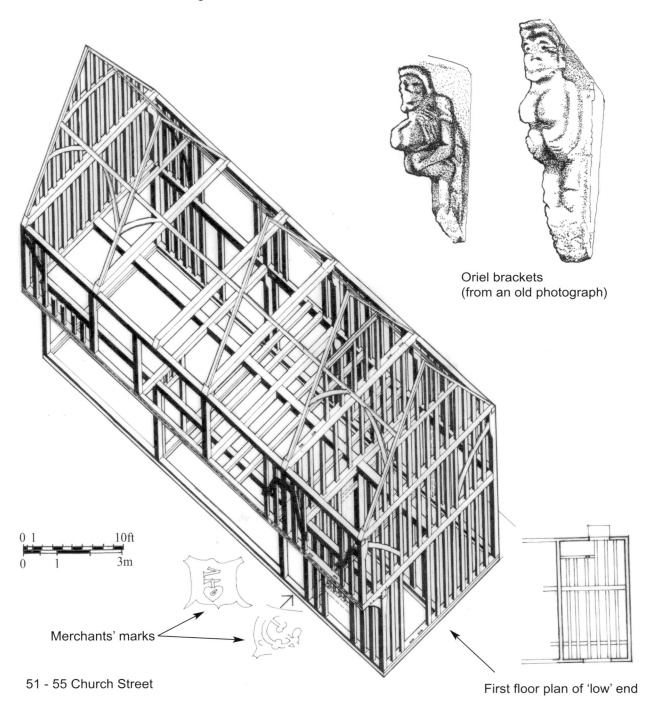

Oriel brackets
(from an old photograph)

Merchants' marks

51 - 55 Church Street

First floor plan of 'low' end

57 Church Street (Hutleys)

This is a baffle (lobby) entrance house of the mid 17th century with a stack-bay and primary bracing. As at The Old Oak (Stoneham Street) there is no contemporary partition between 'the hall' and the south-western bay. The stack has back-to-back fireplaces and there is a fine wall painting of a vase of tulips on the stack facing the upper chamber. The front has a jetty fascia with multiple, simple, mouldings. The rear wing may be contemporary or a slightly later extension. The floor joists over the forward part of the hall are moulded and reused from elsewhere.

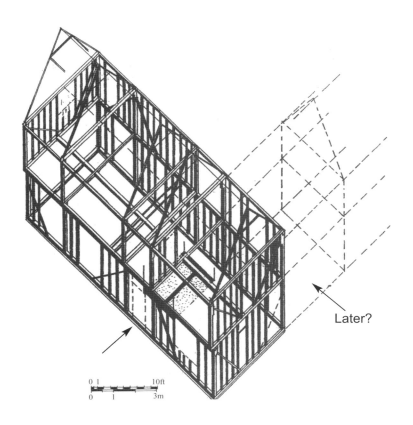

Later?

0 1   10ft
0   1   3m

Off Vane Lane

A small, probably 15th century, cross-wing
in a remote location with regards to the main
concentration of the building frontage.
However, there is a 17th century house
nearby that has not been surveyed.

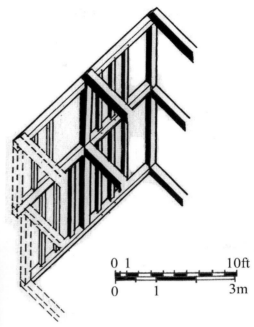

Group of properties between Vane Lane and nos. 75 - 77 Church Street

This axonometric drawing is based on a number of old photographs. It shows
one long-wall jetty house, cross-wings of varying width, and several short
lengths of former open hall. This part of the street probably once consisted
of a series of in-line houses which were later improved through the
superimposition of two-storey cross-wings. The large eastern cross-wing
seems to have been jettied on two sides, to take advantage of a
set-back in the street line. The angling of the boundaries
probably reflects the pre-existing extent of an area
described as 'Church Ponds' in the 1575
survey. All these properties, extending on to
the rear of the Woolpack Inn, had small
separately defined plots of land to the rear
called gardens in the survey. It is possible
that these were abandoned early house
plots and formed the original frontage of
Church Street.

75 - 77 Church Street

A building with a complicated history, it started life as a single-ended, in–line hall house, probably of the 15th century. An old photograph depicts it as a long-wall jetty structure of three storeys with a hipped roof. The existing floor joists above the ground floor are chamfered, suggesting that the upper part of the structure was added in the mid 16th century. Sometime in the 20th century, the upper two floors were removed and the third floor timbers reused to form the present second floor. The original open hall was of about 260 sq. ft. The surviving front elevation contains part of the original door head and jamb, and a 17th century window replacing the original hall window. Evidence suggests that there was a second similar in-line building abutting the western gable. Such pairs of buildings often imply a speculative undertaking.

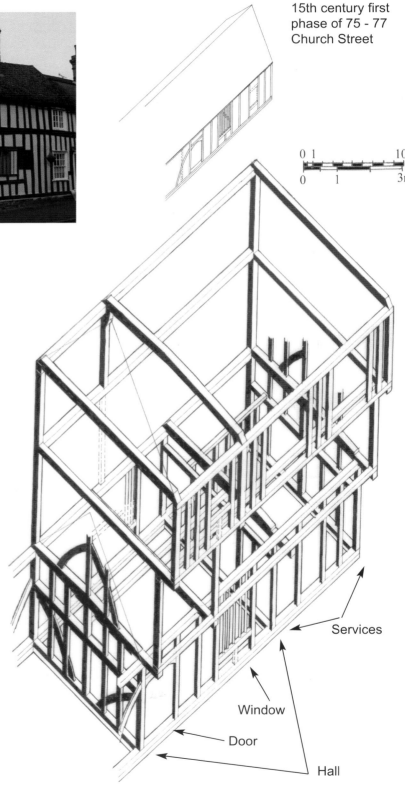

15th century first phase of 75 - 77 Church Street

Services

Window

Door

Hall

91 Church Street (The Woolpack)

The Woolpack is a well-known building which has been published by Cecil Hewett amongst others. It is a good example of a large amount of accommodation being provided on a restricted site. To the east, or right hand side, is a 14th century cross-wing, which was joined to the hall to the west. The hall and cross-wing are probably late 15th century, with a slightly later inserted floor in the hall. The hall is of 260 sq. ft. excluding the undershot cross-passage in the wing to the west. To the rear, in an unconventional location, is a parlour block which prevented any light entering the rear of the hall, which therefore was provided with a large oriel window. A second oriel window was added above after the first floor was inserted. A double oriel, each different in width, is an unusual arrangement. The front bay of the western cross-wing contains a contemporary shop, one of the most complete and attractive examples in East Anglia. The joists of the cross-wing are jointed into the jetty bressumer, an early example of this construction. The wing behind the western cross-wing was jettied on its flank and may have contained the services and/or commercial premises.

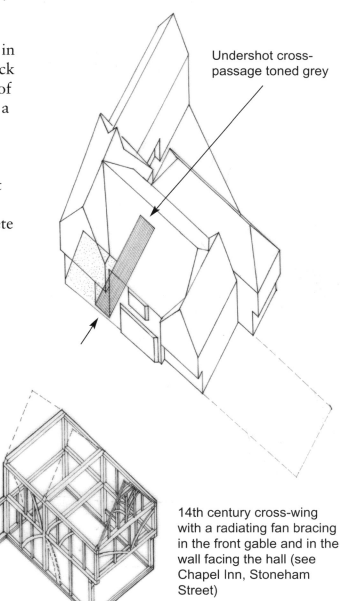

Undershot cross-passage toned grey

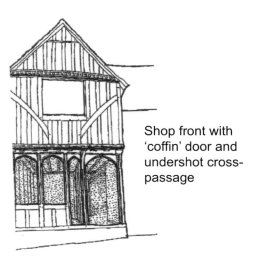

Shop front with 'coffin' door and undershot cross-passage

14th century cross-wing with a radiating fan bracing in the front gable and in the wall facing the hall (see Chapel Inn, Stoneham Street)

0 1   10ft

0   1   3m

CHURCH STREET - SOUTH SIDE

6 Church Green

One jowled post and part of a tie-beam are now attached to the flank of a 17th century house. This building was once part of 'Church Row' which is shown on an early 18th century map. This small fragment suggests a small aisled hall, probably of the early 14th century and likely to have been a part of the early Coggeshall settlement. There is a mortice for an arcade brace, which by its location, suggests a modestly sized hall.

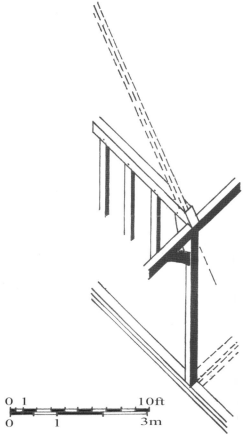

82 Church Street (Coggeshall House)

Coggeshall House is an impressive neo-Jacobean house of the late 19th century. The building contains a number of timber-framed elements that could well have been deliberately retained to retain a sense of continuity. There are single flank walls of three cross-wings, so that some idea of the overall group can be imagined. There is a more complete structure between two of these flanks, with remarkable, thick, ogee braces in the upper walls. At first sight these look 14th century, like at 'Spooners'

Reconstruction of complex

further down the street. However, these are 'primary braces' interrupting the braces, not usually a 14th century feature. It seems probable that this odd structure is contemporary with its first floor and belongs to the late 16th century. It is possible that this structure was built on top of an earlier hall. There is a singular lack of other evidence and it remains somewhat mysterious. The central cross-wing flank has a superimposed tie-beam that has probably been moved from the front.

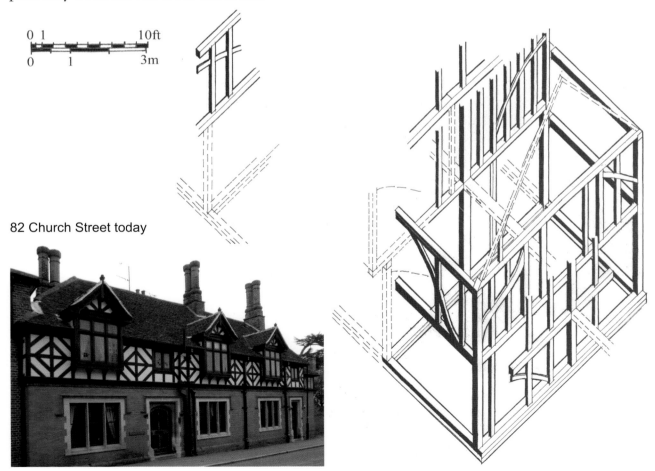

0 1   10ft
0   1   3m

82 Church Street today

64 Church Street

A 15th century jettied two-bay cross-wing with undershot cross-passage. The site subdivisions suggest that it was single-ended and that there may have been other similar units.

62 - 68 Church Street

56 Church Street

To the east is a three-bay cross-wing that has been truncated at the rear and much altered. It probably had a shop in the front bay, with an adjoining passage through to the rear. It seems relatively early with a crown-post roof. To the west is a two-bay late 15th century house. It was three-storey with two jetties, and probably had a pair of gables to the front. There is an undershot cross-passage with speres and studs to the hall. Spine beams are moulded and the carpentry is high quality. As is usually the case in Coggeshall, the third floor is now missing!

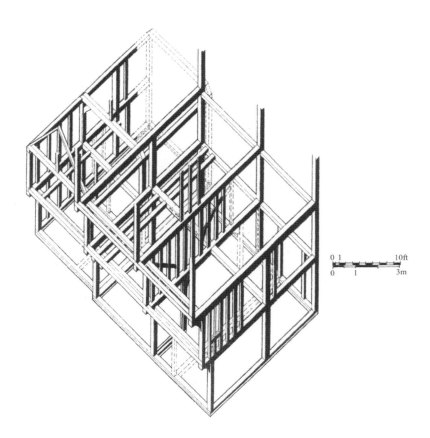

54 - 52 Church Street

The date 1565 is to be found on the carved and moulded fascia of this single-ended long-wall jetty house. The fascia has been shortened at one end, and the date is too early for the building. It may have fitted the adjoining 1 Albert Place where its size and date are a better fit. There is an interesting group of three decorative door openings which suggest a cross-passage against the eastern end. At the western end, there is a stack bay with a relatively complete small room with a door forward of the stack. The north-east end was probably intended as a parlour with a solar above. The rear building is probably contemporary. It has the appearance of a solar wing and has elaborate oriel windows and this seems to duplicate the bay on the frontage. The side boundaries of the site are slightly angled, something echoed by the extension, which could suggest early street encroachment. The hall is of 380 sq. ft. excluding the stack bay.

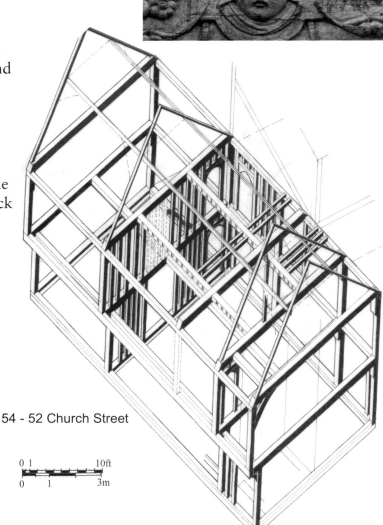

Detail of bressumer

Rear of 54 - 52

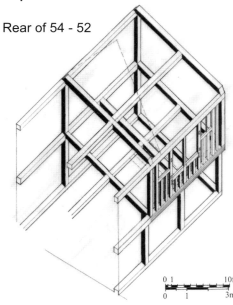

54 - 52 Church Street

0 1   10ft
0   1   3m

0 1   10ft
0   1   3m

32

1 Albert Place (corner with Church Street)

One end of a late 16th-century long wall jetty house with extremely substantial bridging joists set at an angle to the frontage. It is of three bays with moulded spine beams, and has a butt purlin roof with wind bracing.

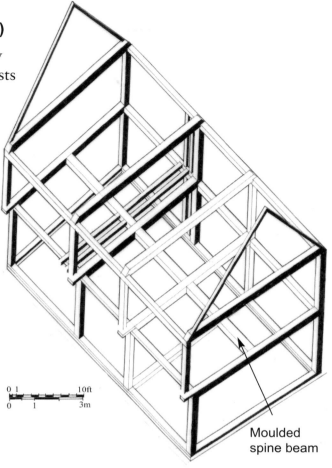

0 1   10ft
0   1   3m

Moulded
spine beam

1 and 3 Albert Place

3 Albert Place

This is a curiously sited small house immediately to the rear of no. 1 and fronting a side lane. It is of two storeys and of three bays with many late 16th century features. The supposed rear elevation has serpentine bracing similar to others in the vicinity. The side purlin roof has raking queen posts, the only example of this fairly common type known in Coggeshall. The southern flank has internal tension braces. It is not known whether this was a single end house or one with a central hall of one bay. (Some of this information is drawn from the statutory list description).

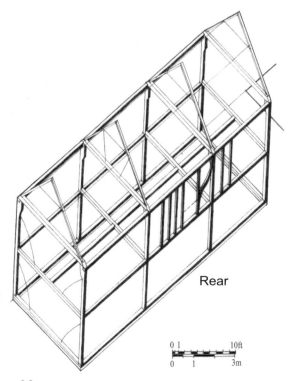

Rear

0 1   10ft
0   1   3m

40 Church Street (Craig Dhu) 1387-1423

This is a small narrow frontage open hall and cross-wing, the front bay of which contained a shop. Unsurprisingly, in view of the restricted site, the cross-passage is undershot, with boarded speres to the hall. There was a seemingly identical unit to the west, of which the flank wall survives. Map evidence suggests no less than six or seven speculative units running up to the present Albert Place, which must have created a striking street scene.

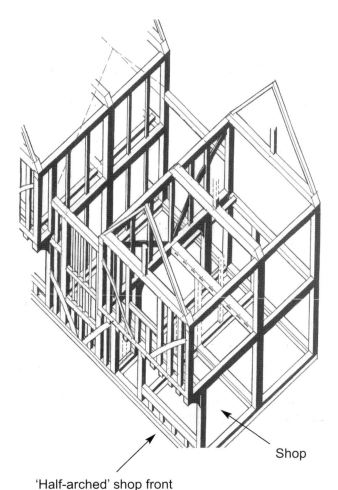

'Half-arched' shop front

Shop

Restored view of frontage

36 Church Street

One flank wall is all that remains of
this much altered house, originally a
narrow two bay cross-winged
building. Attached to it at high level
are the remains of a 14th century
building with parts of a pair of
unusually large braces. These appear
to be curved passing braces which, if
correct, would be unique. The slight
evidence available could be
interpreted to suggest there was a base
cruck hall with braces in the end wall
of the hall corresponding to the base
crucks. These were probably braces
radiating from the backs of the
passing braces but only one can be
seen now.

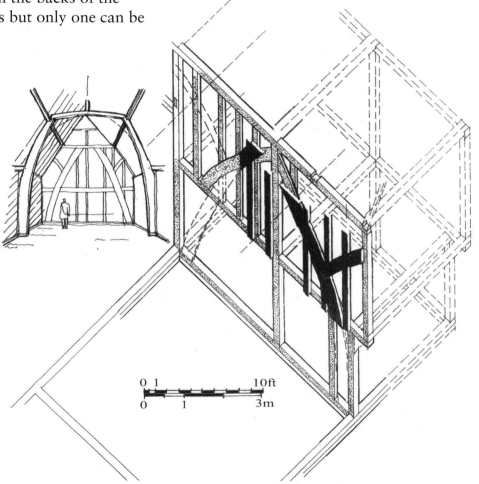

32-34 Church Street (Conservative Club)

A two storied building of three relatively equal bays. Probably of the late 16th century, it gained an extra storey in the 17th century. This is unlikely to be a domestic building and has walls of insubstantial, but close, studwork. Today much is concealed, excepting areas of substantial chamfered main framing.

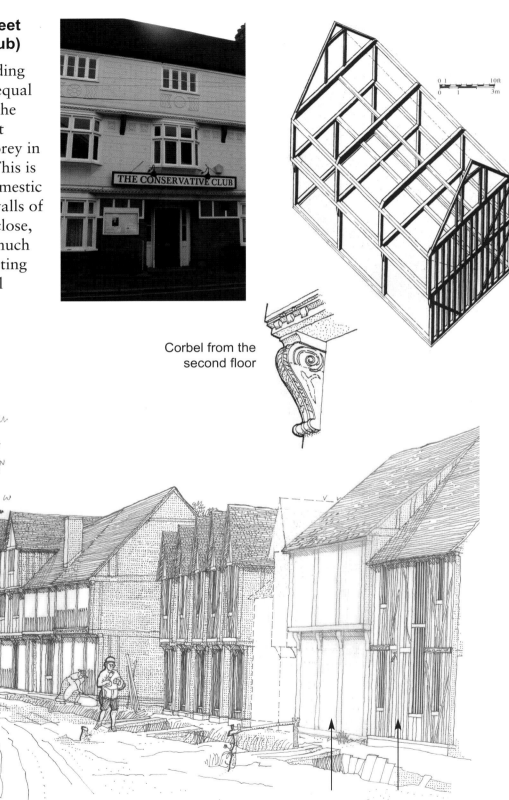

Corbel from the second floor

Church Street   Conservative Club   Spooners

30 Church Street (Spooners) 1353-86

This is a remarkably large in-line house with a
two-bay open hall, though its eastern low end
flank is missing, having been encroached upon
in the 16th century. The front elevation is
distinctive, with an unusual door head and
heavy serpentine braces. There were probably
other such braces in the front and rear
elevations. The hall had a bench recess (now
altered) at the high end, with an ogee headed

door into the parlour. There was a single service room, with a central door and a chamber
over, which was reached by a ladder from the hall. The roof is made of reused timbers from
an earlier hall. The front elevation seems to have had planted fascias at first floor to mimic
the appearance of cross-wings. The parlour/solar wing to the rear is late 16th century.

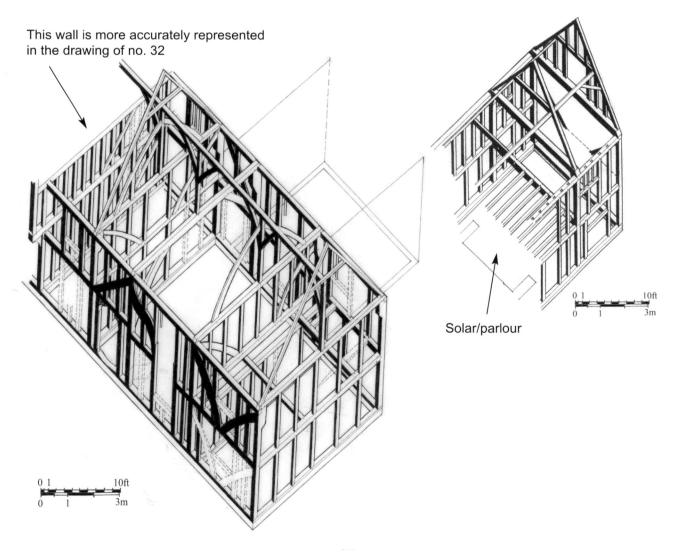

This wall is more accurately represented
in the drawing of no. 32

Solar/parlour

28 Church Street (former Greyhound PH)

Late 16th century long-wall jetty building of two unequal bays. It has jowled posts and a rear wall stack in the north-east corner of the larger bay, possibly identifiable as a hall. The rear wall also has an internal arch brace. Probably a domestic building, with doors through the partitions on both floors.

 To the rear is an earlier, two-bay building, jettied on its south-western flank, of a single chamber on each floor with a central, well-cambered tie beam and chamfered crown-post. The south-west wall has evidence for a window with a shutter guide still in place. This rear 'extension' clearly belonged to an earlier frontage building.

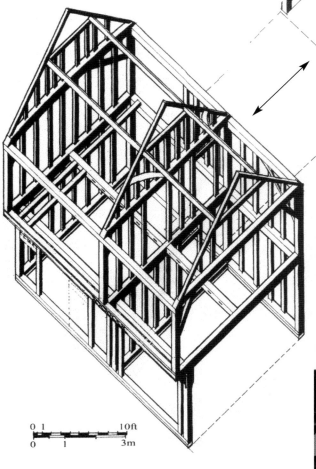

Window

24 Church Street

One narrow bay survives as a 'Wealden' style building.
It is likely to have been a 'single-ender' and the site
dimensions suggest one of a speculative pair. These
type of units usually include a shop and it is likely that
this is the case here. The carpentry suggests the 15th
century. The front top plate brace is of the solid knee
kind.

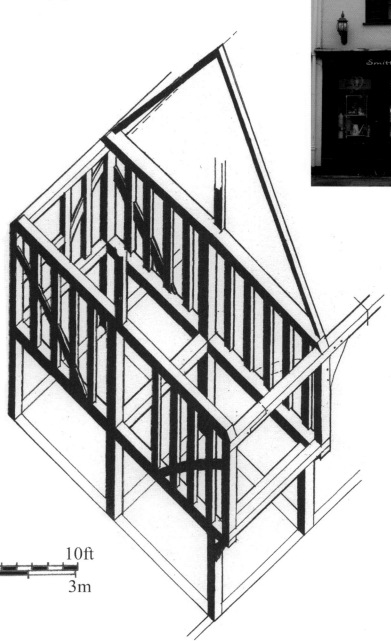

0 1   10ft

0   1   3m

Rear of 18 Church Street

Two-storey rectangular building with floor of substantial joists, that seem to have been shaped from even larger timbers. There seems to have been a door opening on the first floor in the western flank. It was possibly a storage building.

This location may have represented the eastern edge of the market place.

16 - 18 Church Street

Later frontage building

Stairs

0 1   10ft
0   1   3m

10 Church Street

This building displays a 16th-century post and
girt on its south-east corner, probably a remnant
of a long-wall jetty building facing on to the
street. These timbers have been incorporated
into a probably 17th century structure with a
substantial rear stair tower. The first-floor
chamber seems remarkably tall. The building
now has an impressive 18th century decorative
brick street elevation. The location of this
seemingly isolated building, probably forward of
the Church Street stream, may indicate that it
was of some community significance.

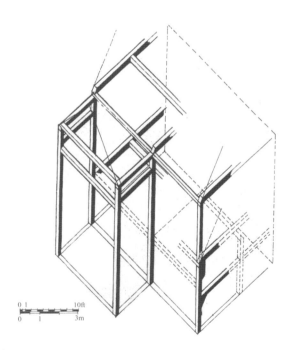

The Church Street walk finishes at 10 Church Street

East Street

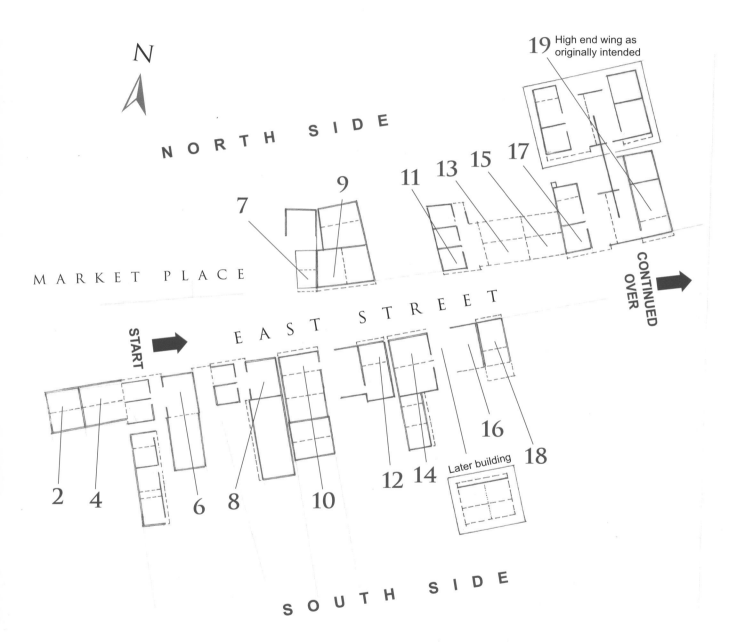

EAST STREET

**The walk begins on the north side of East Street
and returns on the south side**

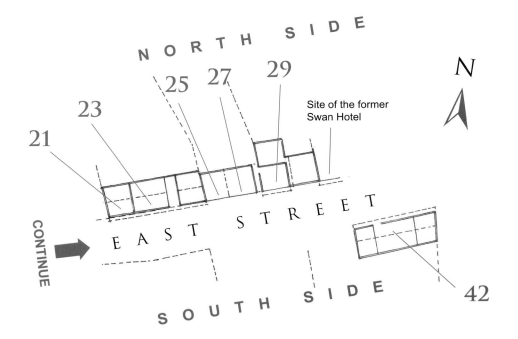

8 East Street reconstruction spere opening to cross-wing

EAST STREET - NORTH SIDE

9 East Street

This is a 17th century long-wall jetty building of two equal undivided bays. To the rear is a slightly later extension making for an L-shaped plan. The front range at ground floor was probably commercial, but soon gained a chimney stack when, perhaps, the entire building became domestic.

To the west (now no. 7) are the remains of two earlier structures that may represent stalls or market structures, sited on and near the main road frontage. It is possible that these may have been moved from elsewhere, in order to provide a consolidated frontage.

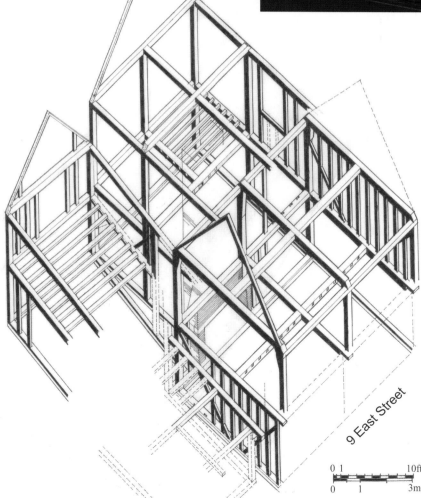

9 East Street

0 1   10ft

0   1   3m

11 - 13 East Street

This is a three bay cross-wing with an undershot cross-passage, dated to 1404-30. There was probably a shop in the front bay. The rear room and the upper floor were accessed via doors from this cross-passage. There are mysterious gaps in the framing of the eastern flank wall at first floor. The rear room of the cross-wing might have been a kitchen as there is an existing chimney stack in the rear wall. To the east (in no. 13) are a pair of posts and tie-beams of a former hall. These have been utilised to provide support for a partition of closely spaced studs. The surviving tie-beam of this hall has mortices for slightly asymmetrical arch-braces, perhaps suggesting a 'Wealden' type roof.

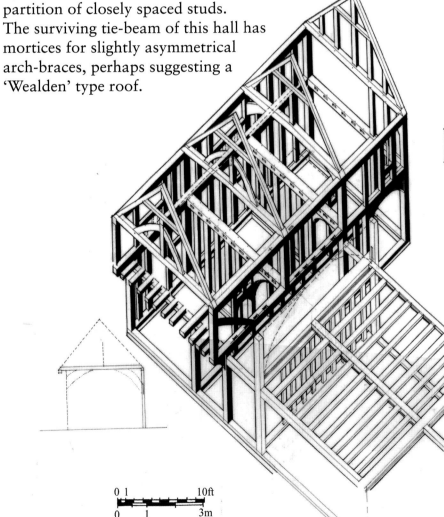

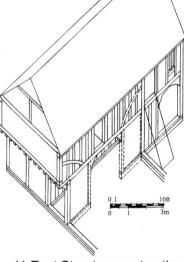

11 East Street reconstruction/ interpretation

15 East Street

This is a single, un-jettied bay of mid-to-late 17th century framing. However, there is a chimney stack of unusual 'nostril type' with extra draught inducing flues of probable c.1600 date which was apparently associated with an earlier phase of construction. This stack may have served a parlour associated with the cross-wing and hall at nos. 11 and 13.

0 1   10ft

0   1   3m

17 - 19 East Street (former Through Inn)

The Through Inn is a full H-plan house with a remarkably wide undershot cross-passage in the service cross-wing, which had a shop in the front bay with a half-arched shop front. On the rear wall, at first floor level, there was a garderobe. The hall is of two extremely unequal bays with, seemingly, only a very small window on the front elevation. It is possible that the house was originally in-line: on this basis, the high end cross-wing looks like a replacement of the eastern parlour bay. This wing was intended to be of only two bays, but a third was introduced, towards the street before the building was erected on the site. Did the builder obtain more land at the rear? The function of the rear bay at ground floor level is unknown, but there was a second garderobe on the floor above it.

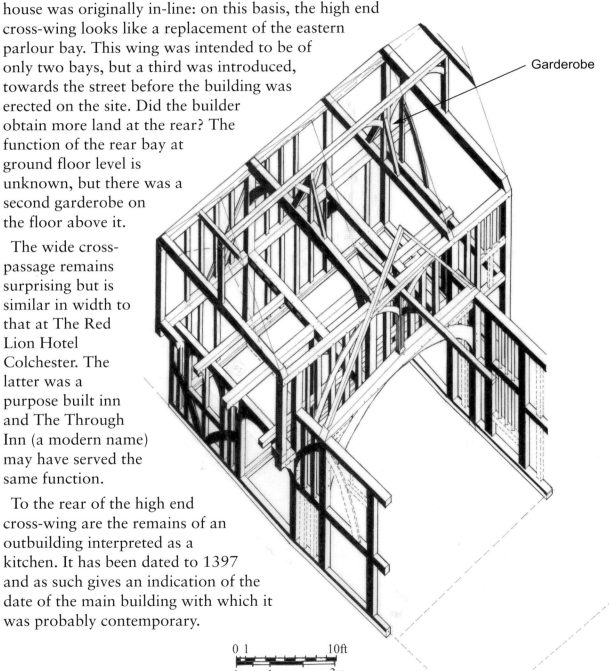

Garderobe

The wide cross-passage remains surprising but is similar in width to that at The Red Lion Hotel Colchester. The latter was a purpose built inn and The Through Inn (a modern name) may have served the same function.

To the rear of the high end cross-wing are the remains of an outbuilding interpreted as a kitchen. It has been dated to 1397 and as such gives an indication of the date of the main building with which it was probably contemporary.

0 1   10ft

0   1   3m

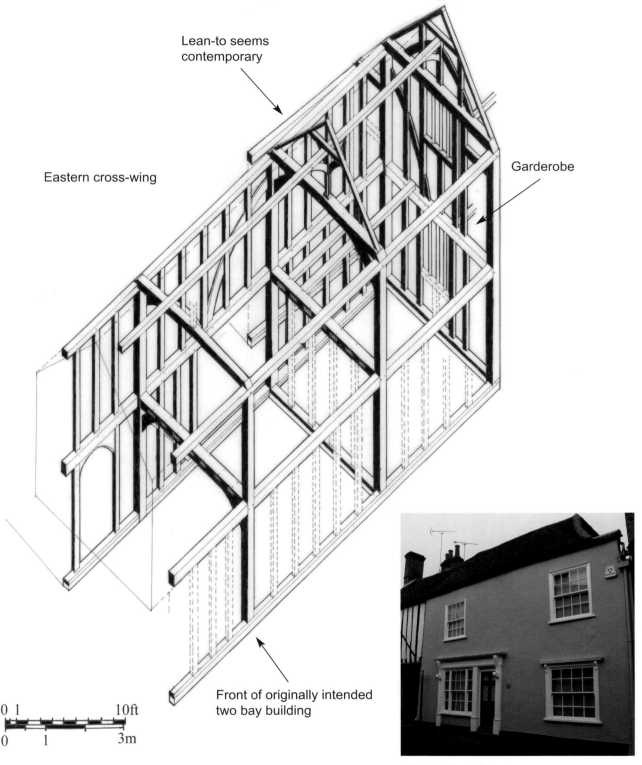

Lean-to seems
contemporary

Eastern cross-wing

Garderobe

Front of originally intended
two bay building

0 1   10ft

0   1   3m

17 - 19 East Street

21 - 23 East Street

This is an exceptionally long jettied six bay house built in 1599. It was probably of lobby-entry plan, with an off centre chimney stack. The chimney was later moved to a central position and the house has suffered multiple sub-divisions, making the plan form difficult to interpret. However, there would seem to have been a hall of two equal bays, and the front elevation had large windows, possibly oriels. There is evidence for a rear door opening at the end of the hall uggesting the possibility of a cross-passage in this traditional, location. The westernmost bay could have been in separate occupation. This was certainly the case in the later 17th century. The 'transitional' plan form could be a curious mixture of traditional and innovation. A later tunnel cut through the stack reflects a later sub-division of the property and its adaptation for use by several households.

0 1 ⊢⊣⊢⊣⊢⊣ 10ft
0   1   3m

23 East Street

Door?

21 East Street

25 - 27 East Street

A two-storey three-bay 17th century building, probably jettied, with some re-used timbers. As originally built, it was probably non-domestic in function. The roof was rebuilt in the 19th century. An access passage at the east end reveals the outer flank of no. 29 and probably relates to an early gap in the frontage.

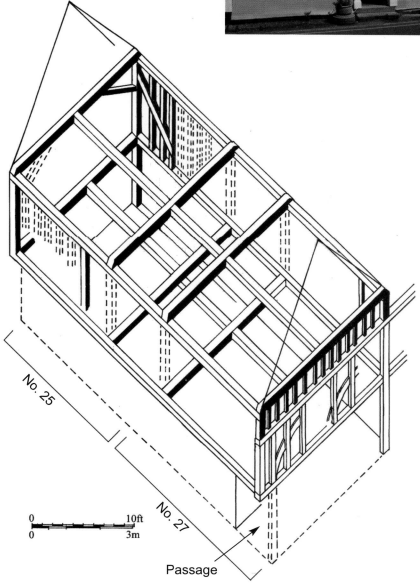

No. 25

No. 27

0   10ft
0   3m

Passage

29 East Street

Only one and a part bay survive of this probable two-bay cross-wing. The front bay was almost certainly a shop. The front elevation has a single groove between each post for some form of shutter. The upper floor was gained by a door and stair on the western flank. The rear bay of the cross-wing was reached by a door from the hall abutting the central post. From close observation it can be inferred that the two-bay hall was originally aisled. Its central tie-beam survives incorporated into a later unaisled replacement. The design of the hall can be recovered from its original top plate which was reused in the ground floor of no. 27 to the west. From this it can also be deduced that the aisled hall was in-line and the cross-wing was a later improvement.

To the east of the existing rebuilt hall are the remains of a further cross-wing, reduced to a single wall which has very close studwork and is of extremely superior carpentry. It has been dated 1418-54. This cross-wing was probably a rebuilding of an in-line end to the aisled hall which would have been from the 14th century. The cross-wing later formed part of the now demolished Swan public house.

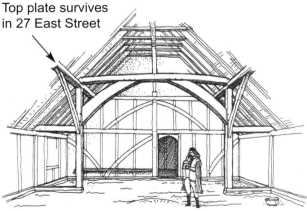

Top plate survives in 27 East Street

Reconstructed interior of aisled hall

0 1   10ft

0   1   3m

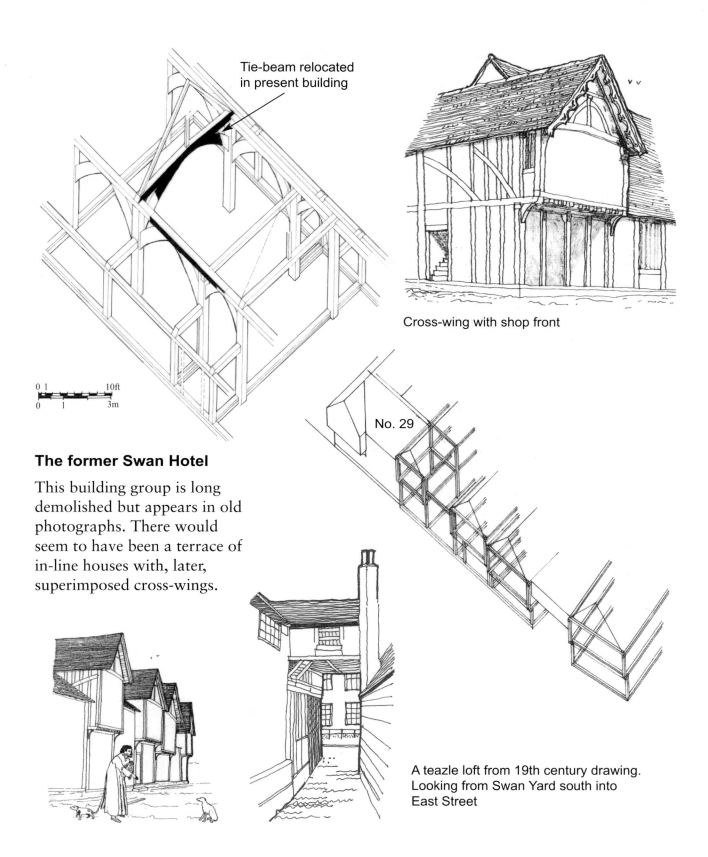

Tie-beam relocated in present building

Cross-wing with shop front

No. 29

The former Swan Hotel

This building group is long demolished but appears in old photographs. There would seem to have been a terrace of in-line houses with, later, superimposed cross-wings.

A teazle loft from 19th century drawing. Looking from Swan Yard south into East Street

53

EAST STREET - SOUTH SIDE

42 East Street

The sketch is based on the statutory list description. It is a 16th century long-wall jetty house of standard plan and of four relatively equal bays. The two central bays formed the hall with the services to the west. There are jowled posts and a crown-post roof with longitudinal braces interrupted by a later chimney stack. At this point in East Street, the frontage pushes forward making the west gable end a conspicuous feature in the townscape.

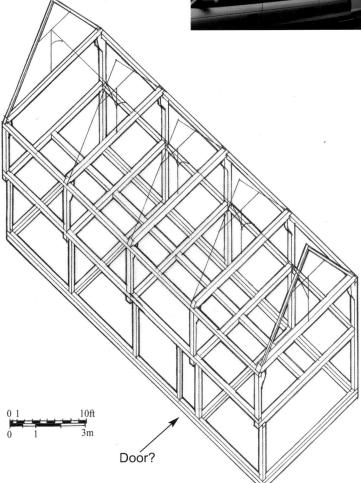

0 1   10ft
0   1   3m

Door?

18 East Street

No. 18 is an extremely tall and narrow cross-wing, surviving only as one bay, and built 1361-97. It is open-framed against the hall which is thought to have existed at no. 16. Its strange proportions may have arisen by it having been a replacement for an 'in-line' end. The internal wall bracing is extremely unusual and it has a large opening for a primitive chimney stack against the east flank. Access between cross-wing and hall is unclear unless there had been a rear aisle (or the tension braces in the side wall were arranged asymmetrically). Stylistically, this cross-wing seems to be at odds with the usual conventions of the local vernacular.

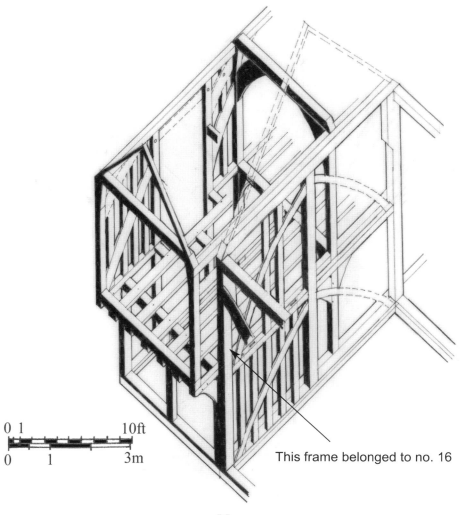

0 1   10ft

0   1   3m

This frame belonged to no. 16

16 East Street (Phase 2)

This is an infill building dated to 1636 that is open-framed against nos. 14 and 18. Even the rear appears to be open-framed, perhaps to a previous aisle wall. The butt purlin roof, with its rafters framed into the purlins, had an off-set dormer to the front. There was a further dormer at the eastern end of the rear which provided for an external rear stair. The double set of butt purlins, with short intervening rafters, is precocious and it more easily allowed the provision of the dormer.

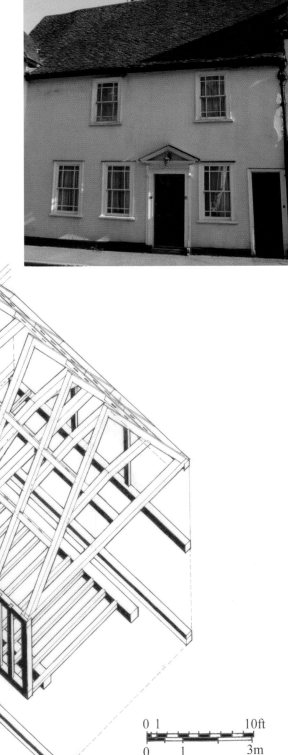

16 East Street (Phase 1)

It is suggested that there was formerly an open hall, probably rear aisled, between nos. 14 and 18. The eastern end wall of this hall survives against the flank of no. 18. It is possible that, as has been previously noted, the low end of this hall functioned as services for no. 14.

14 East Street

At first sight this looks like an extremely elegant and expensive cross-wing, which has been dated to 1435. However, despite the pair of doors in the side wall, there are no indications of a service sub-division and the central bridging joist is boldly moulded. It is possible that it was a ground floor hall of precocious intent, with a lofty chamber above, in which case the services were presumably to the east.

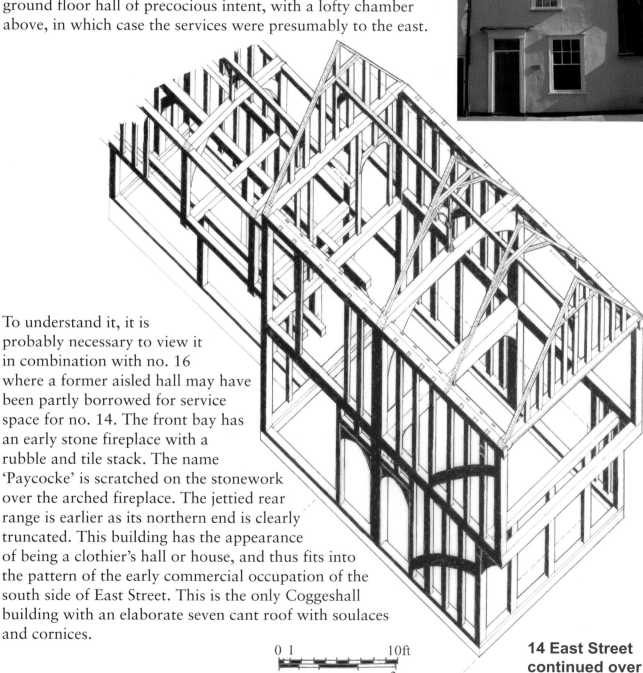

To understand it, it is probably necessary to view it in combination with no. 16 where a former aisled hall may have been partly borrowed for service space for no. 14. The front bay has an early stone fireplace with a rubble and tile stack. The name 'Paycocke' is scratched on the stonework over the arched fireplace. The jettied rear range is earlier as its northern end is clearly truncated. This building has the appearance of being a clothier's hall or house, and thus fits into the pattern of the early commercial occupation of the south side of East Street. This is the only Coggeshall building with an elaborate seven cant roof with soulaces and cornices.

0 1   10ft
0   1   3m

**14 East Street
continued over**

14 East Street continued

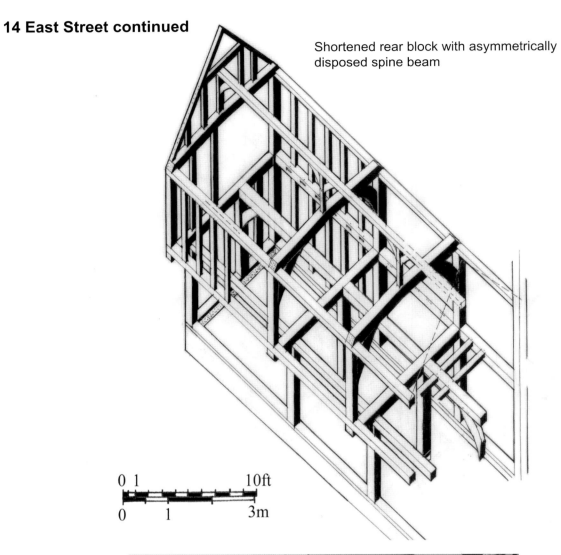

Shortened rear block with asymmetrically disposed spine beam

0 1   10ft

0   1   3m

18 - 14 East Street

12 East Street

This is a two-bay high-end cross-wing with a very deep rear bay. The hall to the west of it only survives as a front top plate (and possibly posts) and may well have had a rear aisle to help accommodate, in the limited space available, both hall and service functions. The high end wall has a probably late example of a fan or radial bracing.

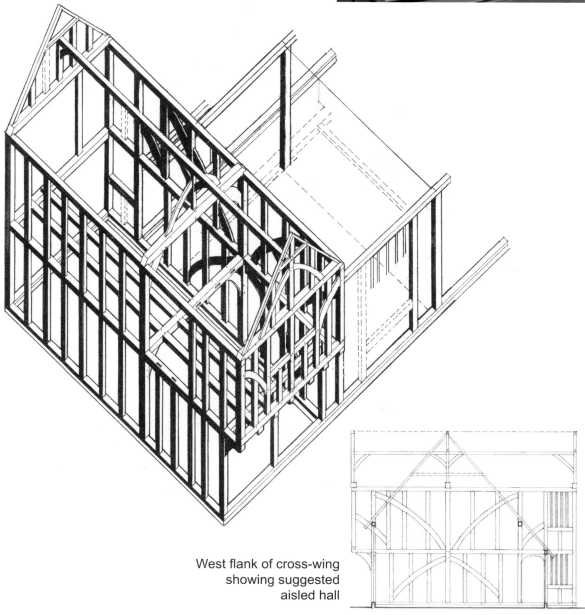

West flank of cross-wing
showing suggested
aisled hall

59

10 East Street

This is a cross-wing like building of three equal bays dated to 1386. On the east flank, there is a door opening, providing access to the stair trap to the first floor. There is no evidence for any internal partitions and a strange central storey post in the rear wall echoes that at 18 Stoneham Street. It is suggested that this building was a 'wool-hall' or 'wool house' without any domestic function. The front bay could possibly have been a shop. To the rear is a two-bay, un-jettied building built of re-used timber. In its present form it is likely to be early 17th century. The moulded floor joists came from a sophisticated 15th/16th century building.

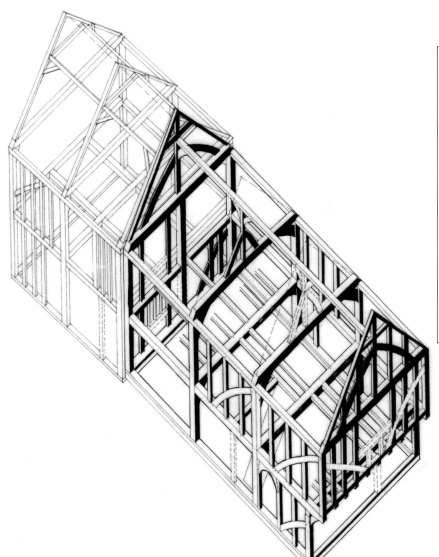

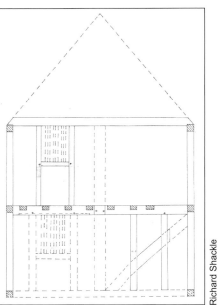

Rear wall of cross-wing

Richard Shackle

8 East Street

A hall and cross-wing complex slightly later (16th century) but similar in size to no. 6. The cross-wing has an undershot cross-passage with formerly vertical boarded speres. Its front bay may have been a shop. Nevertheless it is more likely a parlour and service room occupied this ground floor as there otherwise would be no location for the former.

Later range

Hall

Speres

0 1   10ft

0   1   3m

**8 East Street
continued over**

8 East Street (second phase)

In 1618 a large two bay structure was erected abutting the rear, with its gabled roof over-sailing the former hall. This is jettied to the west with a moulded inner bressumer. A dropped tie-beam arrangement allowed a low storage loft and there is a mixture of internal and primary braces. It is likely that this combination represents a particular stage in the evolution of framing technique. The west front had large upper floor windows (probably oriels) and there is notable evidence for a wide shallow ground floor window, with numerous diamond mullions. It seems likely that this phase involves primarily domestic use, but with important secondary commercial activity. The internal bracing was intended to look smart and impressive, suitable for a domestic environment. It is possible this long wing at right angles to East Street replaced an earlier commercial range like those at no. 6.

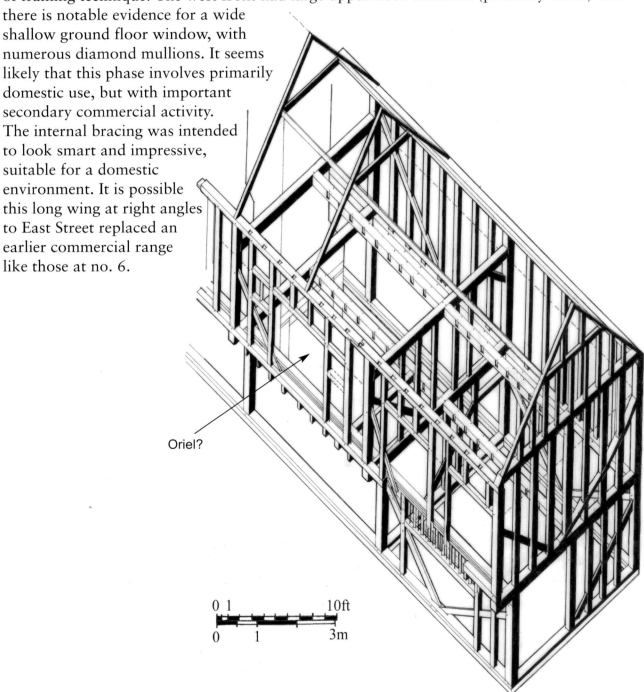

Oriel?

0 1   10ft

0   1   3m

6 East Street

This is a site and buildings with a complex history. The land, leading down to the river, could well have been used for processing for the clothing industry. The earliest surviving structure (1441) seems to have been a workshop with large, plain, windows opening under an east-facing jetty. The site also held a single storey detached building with an elaborate window in its west flank. It seems probable that the previously mentioned workshop, originally extended further to the north as some major structural members seem to extend in this direction.

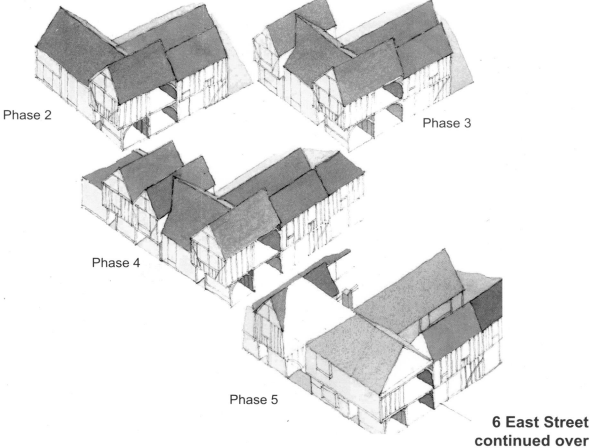

6 East Street sequence

Phase 1

Phase 2

Phase 3

Phase 4

Phase 5

**6 East Street
continued over**

6 East Street continued

Later in the 15th century, a house was built on the frontage and the workshop block shortened to provide the space. This house has a two-bay, jettied, cross-wing, with undershot cross-passage and small hall. It is suggested that it also had an in-line end, extending to the eastern site boundary.

The front room of the cross-wing, was obviously a shop with mortices surviving for its arched frontage. The floor joists were jointed into the moulded front bressumer, as at The Woolpack (Church Street).

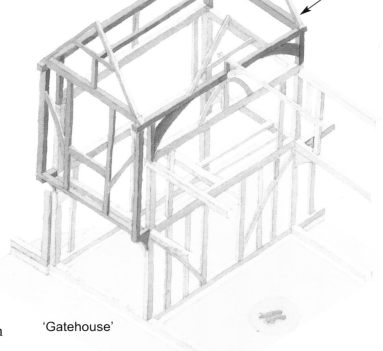

'Imposed' cross-wing

'Gatehouse'

A little later, the 'in-line end' had a new first floor, of jettied cross-wing character, imposed on top. Later still, the ground floor room was largely removed, to form the 'gatehouse' mentioned in documentary sources. The much earlier, detached block then was incorporated into the frontage house probably to make a parlour. In the late 16th century the hall was floored and an extra storey was added above the parlour. The new chamber, above the hall, was given a fireplace with stone surround. Probably also in the 17th century, the 'gatehouse' was demolished leaving the existing narrow lane down to the river.

At some time in the 15th century, a curious building was erected, south of the original workshop block. This also has an east facing jettied flank and incorporates a near central, timber chimney-stack. In its present form, it has a semi-basement but this is probably a later change. It is however possible that this little building was a dye house and if so, is a remarkable survivor of an unusual building type.

There are further buildings, some with reused moulded floor joists, further to the south, but these defy explanation.

The above description is extremely hypothetical and only the best that can be offered with our present knowledge. Clearly there was rapid change at the site and its structures were speedily adapted to suit changing circumstances.

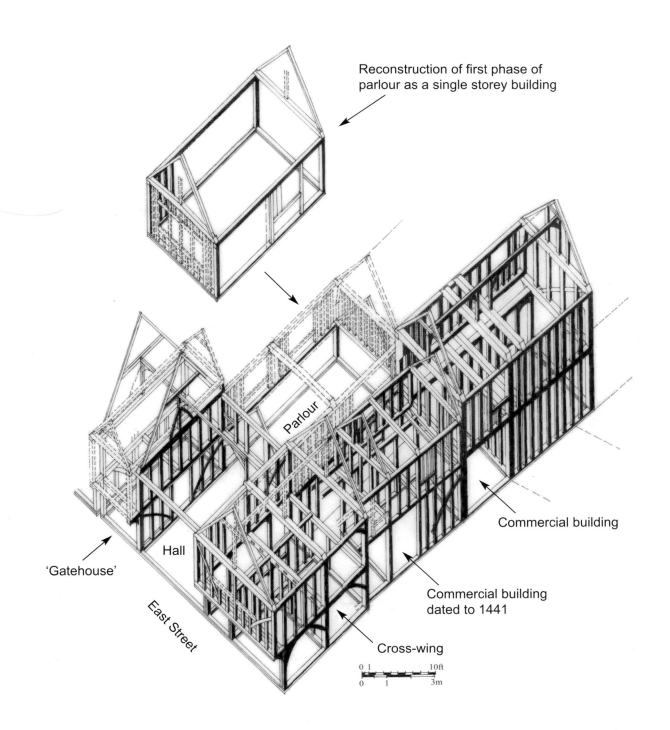

Reconstruction of first phase of parlour as a single storey building

Parlour

'Gatehouse'

Hall

East Street

Cross-wing

Commercial building

Commercial building dated to 1441

0 1   10ft
0   1   3m

6 East Street
continued over

Rear of 6 East Street

To the rear of the previously mentioned workshop, there is a two storey structure, now with a sub-basement. Jettied to the east, it is of two bays sandwiching a timber framed chimney stack, probably with a louvre on top. This is a rare surviving industrial structure and the two doorways suggest also a minor domestic function. The varied buildings on the site of no. 6 indicate that it was being put to commercial, either rented out or directly by its owner. In the late 16th century, it belonged to Robert Litherland, a prominent clothier.

Reconstruction view of rear yard with 'dyehouse' and workshop - parallel block shown with dashed line

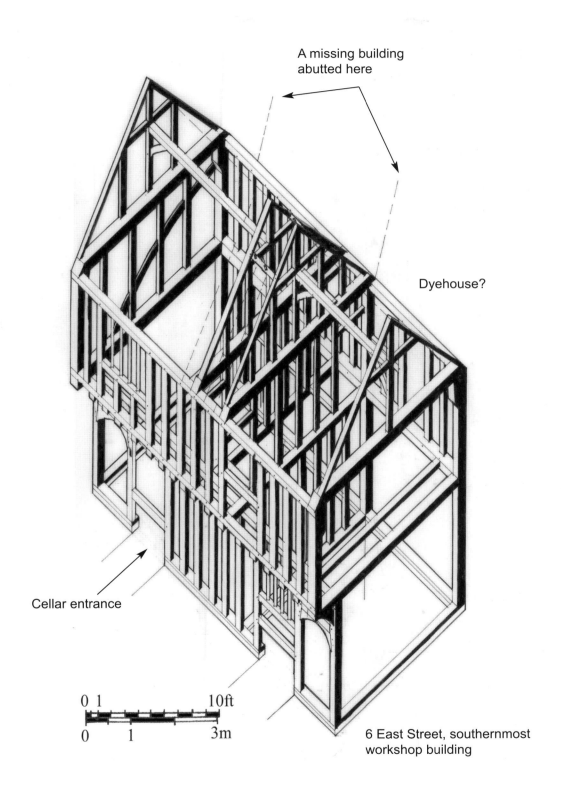

A missing building
abutted here

Dyehouse?

Cellar entrance

0 1   10ft

0 1   3m

6 East Street, southernmost
workshop building

2 - 4 East Street

This is a 17th century lobby-entry house arranged about a central chimney stack but now divided into two dwellings. Much of the timber frame is covered, but there are jowled storey posts and the walls are made with close studding with primary braces. The roof is of clasped purlin construction. There is evidence for a centrally located stair tower to the rear, opposite the chimney, and to the east for a floored building which was probably a kitchen.

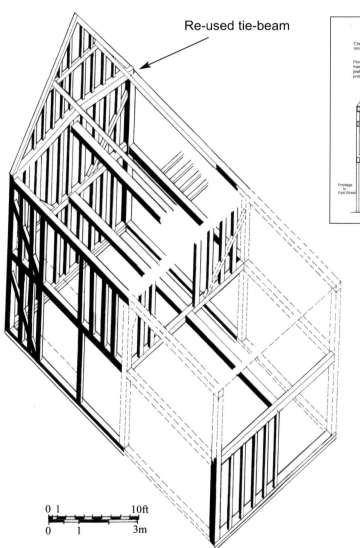

Re-used tie-beam

0 1   10ft

0   1   3m

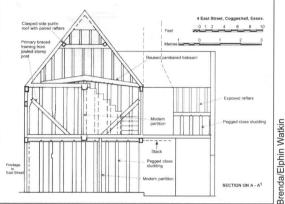

The East Street walk finishes at 2 - 4 East Street

68

WEST STREET

**The walk begins on the south side of West Street
and returns on the north side**

N

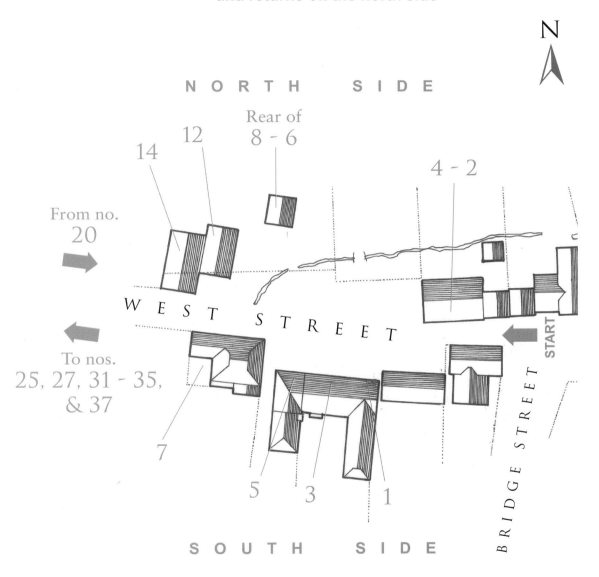

NORTH   SIDE

Rear of
8 - 6

14

12

4 - 2

From no.
20

W E S T   S T R E E T

To nos.
25, 27, 31 - 35,
& 37

7

5   3   1

BRIDGE STREET

START

SOUTH   SIDE

West Street viewed from the White Hart

WEST STREET - SOUTH SIDE

1 West Street

Behind the 'end' of the building, discussed below, is a later structure, the building of which required the removal of the service lean-to. This is of early to mid 17th century and of three equal bays. It would seem to be a commercial block, possibly for storage, with primary bracing and strongly arched collars. The south end is hipped with a small gable. The drawing duplicates the 'end' as depicted in the following illustration.

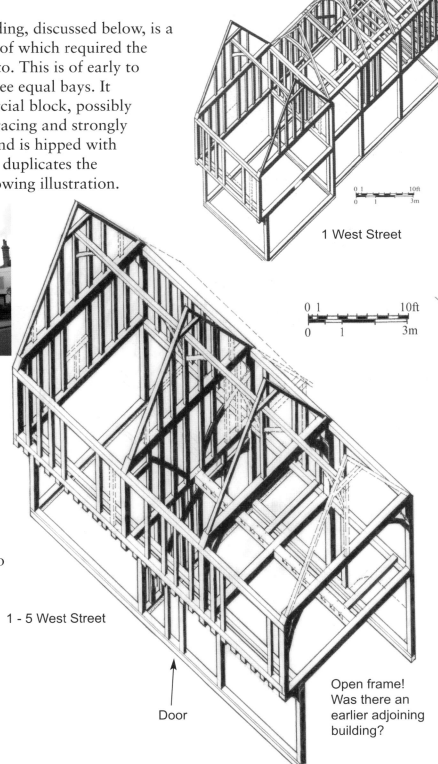

0 1   10ft
0   1   3m

1 West Street

1 - 5 West Street

A three-bay single ended house of the early 16th century. The hall is of two equal bays with a cross-passage at the eastern end. The location of the service doors shows that there was probably an aisle-like, lean-to behind the eastern bay, to provide sufficient space for a large parlour and one service room.

0 1   10ft
0   1   3m

1 - 5 West Street

Door

Open frame! Was there an earlier adjoining building?

5 West Street

In the late 16th century, this site seems to have been vacant ground. However today there are on the frontage the remains of an ancient looking two storey frame, with a later, possibly 18th century, floor. It seems likely that this is part of a building re-located from elsewhere. To the rear of this fragment, is a two-bay domestic unit of the early 17th century. It has jowled posts and primary bracing between posts and plates, and a contemporary chimney stack.

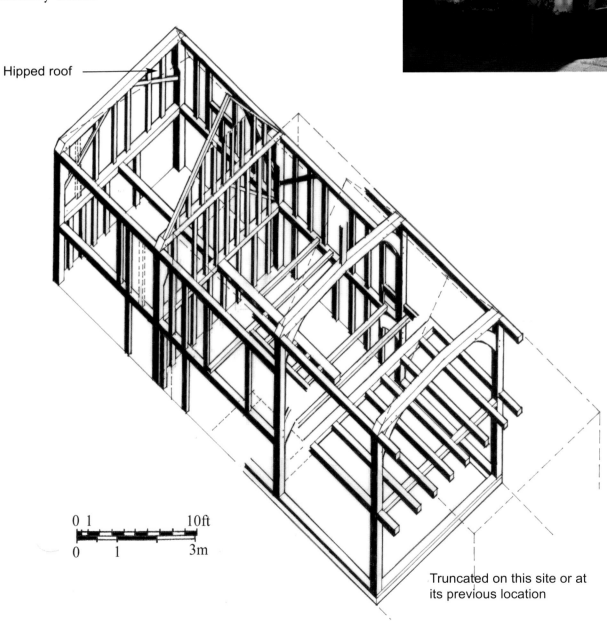

Hipped roof

0 1　　　　　　10ft
0　　1　　3m

Truncated on this site or at its previous location

7 West Street

(The former Cricketers Public House)

Originally built as the manorial court hall
c.1403-29, this is a square two storey building
jettied to the north. It is a remarkable survivor
of an interesting building type. The court hall
itself is a two bay first floor room, surmounted
by a pyramidal roof. Original access was by a
door in the south west corner, probably via an
outside staircase. At this corner a two storey
stair tower was later added, with a first floor
balcony and a little contemporary shop
underneath.

The ground floor has wide multi-mullioned
windows and a big central door on the northern
street elevation, which is now concealed by a
Georgian brick facade. The ground floor
elevation at the rear has also seen changes
which finally took the form of a single wide
opening. There is slight evidence of a further
structure which may have comprised a pentice
roof. It is known that the building was used as
the shambles and the pentice and wide opening
may relate to this use.

Court room on first floor

7 West Street continued

West Street reconstructed view with the former Cricketers ahead

7 West Street continued

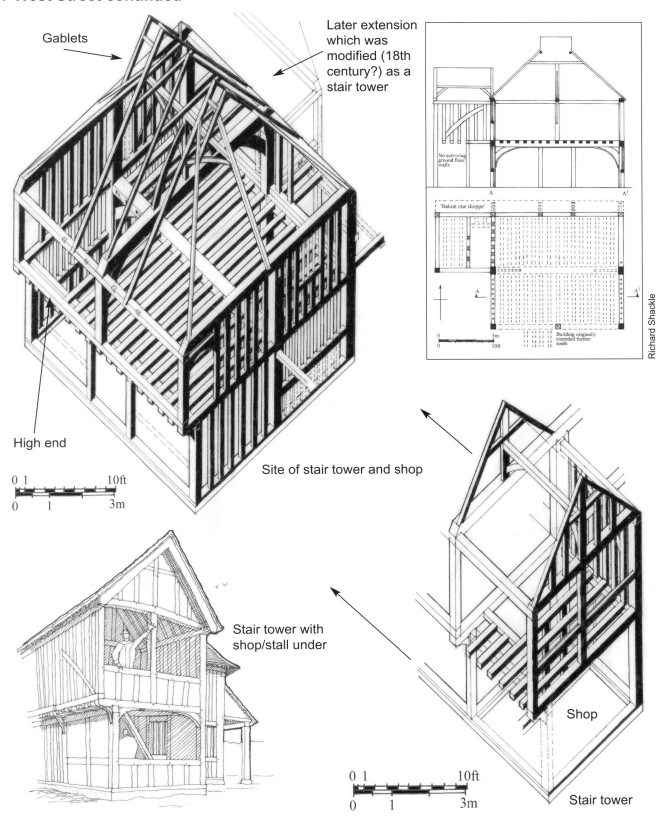

Gablets

Later extension which was modified (18th century?) as a stair tower

High end

Site of stair tower and shop

Stair tower with shop/stall under

Shop

Stair tower

No surviving ground floor walls

A   A¹

'Bakon one shoppe'

Building originally extended further south

Richard Shackle

25 West Street (Paycockes House)

This well known National Trust property is difficult to interpret and has tested the brains of numerous experts, none of whom have reached an entirely satisfactory conclusion. All that can be offered is a speculative explanation of it that best suits the surviving evidence. It seems a good example of building as an expression of special circumstances at a particular moment in time.

Documentary sources indicate that the Paycocke family owned a house on this site prior to its construction in 1509. It was bequeathed to Thomas Paycocke by his father John in his will proved in 1506. It is suggested that this took the form of an in-line house, at right angles to the West Street frontage. This curious siting may have been related to a lane running south to the river in the valley. In the 15th century the high end to the south was rebuilt as the two-storey jettied block that partially survives at the rear of the house today.

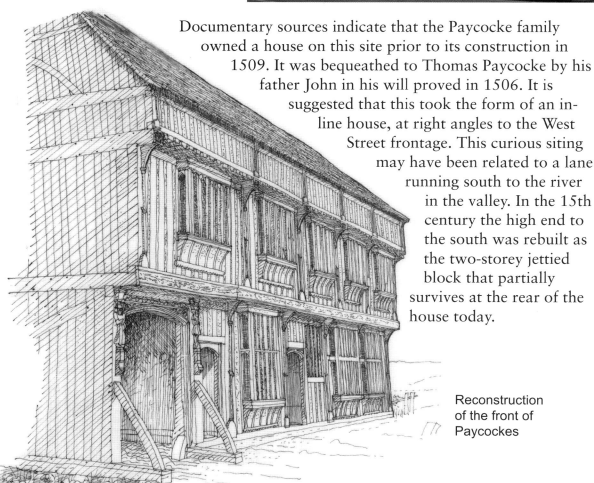

Reconstruction of the front of Paycockes

When Thomas Paycocke came to rebuild, he retained the old hall, effectively as an attached kitchen or servants' hall. This arrangement determined the unusual plan form of his new house, which otherwise was designed to display his wealth and status.

In many ways, it is a traditional cross-passage house, but with the service room and parlour swapping places, so that the passage is next to the parlour as opposed to the usual position next to the service room. This transposition was necessitated by the position of the old hall, and the need to connect it to the new display hall and narrow single service room.

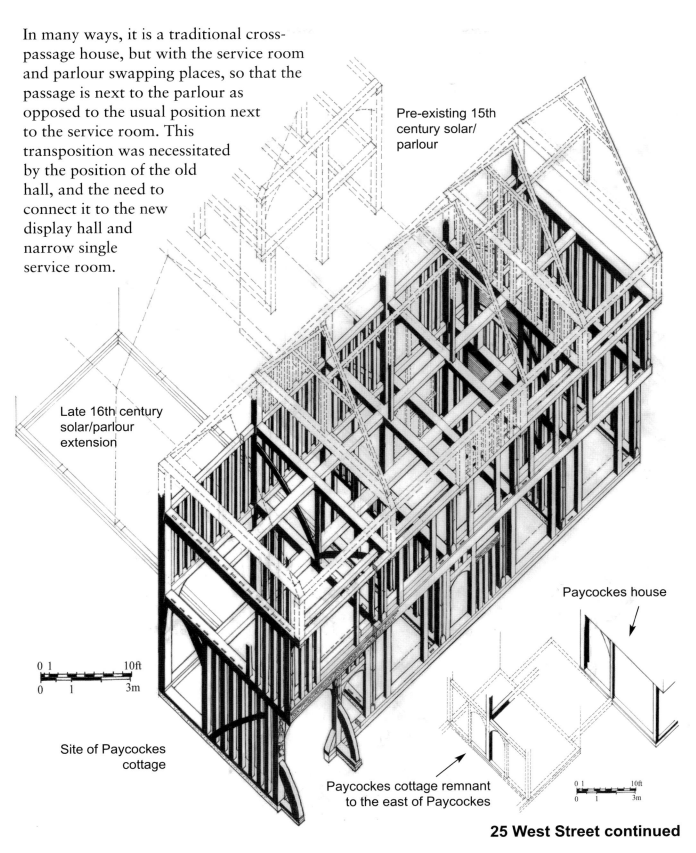

Pre-existing 15th century solar/parlour

Late 16th century solar/parlour extension

Paycockes house

Site of Paycockes cottage

Paycockes cottage remnant to the east of Paycockes

0 1   10ft

0   1   3m

25 West Street continued

25 West Street continued

The one truly innovative feature was a long storage loft at second floor over the entire range. Attics were not popular in Essex for at least another 60 years, and parallels with French buildings come to mind. Paycockes is thus the first known building to give architectural expression to the clothier's need for storage.

This top attic floor was for some reason removed in the late 16th century. There is some charring of the upper timbers towards the east end which could represent a roof fire. It is now impossible to determine the precise design of the original roof although the much later attic at the adjacent Fleece public house probably mirrors its profile. The only comparable local one is the former Bonners in North Hill, Colchester, where the true attic floor is earlier and more complicated and experimental looking.

The east bay with the carriage arch was a later alteration. The building was however designed to provide the extra length to accommodate the arch and so it was probably always planned. Surprisingly internal access from the solar over the arch was not foreseen and a doorway had to be broken through a neatly framed wall. Possibly this was the result of second thoughts, the room originally being intended to be detached. It could be that the elaborate doorway on the ground floor was first intended to lead to a stair to the upper chamber. A business use seems likely for the end upper bay and an imposing doorway would probably have been considered necessary.

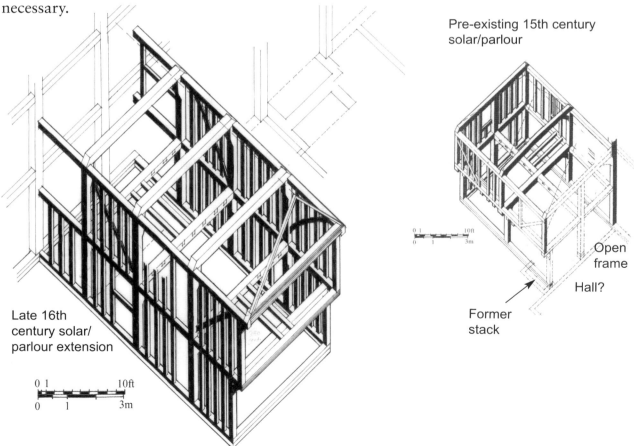

Pre-existing 15th century solar/parlour

Open frame

Hall?

Former stack

Late 16th century solar/ parlour extension

0 1   10ft
0   1   3m

0 1   10ft
0   1   3m

The other unexplained mystery of Paycockes house is the superimposed fireplaces in the hall west wall. This wall of carefully designed framing has been disturbed but insufficiently to reveal its original construction. However there are no signs of a chimney stack and no way for smoke to exit. It has been suggested that they were dummy stacks simply to impress visitors.

Ground floor 'fireplace'

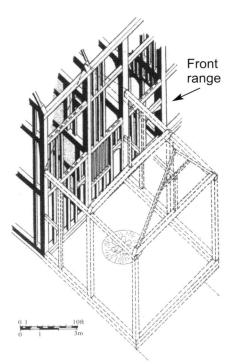

Front range

Rear of south-west corner with suggested, former, open hall

Rear of Paycockes today

Rear of Paycockes mid 16th century. The garden is a working area

Despite its unusual design and elaborate features, Paycockes still looks the product of local carpentry, enhanced by the skills of a specialist carver and moulder. The use of brick nogging in the studwork, otherwise unknown at Coggeshall, is a high status practice of the time. There can be no doubt that Paycockes would have impressed local people and influenced later buildings in the town.

25 West Street continued

Thomas Paycocke's intended dwelling?

In its present form the internal partition of the house with superimposed fireplaces is not logical. It seems possible that this two storied assembly was intended to be the western timber wall of the building. Beyond this would have been a brick chimney stack of the zonal brickwork type of which a slightly later type can be seen at Aldeburgh Moot Hall.

It is possible that there was a change of plan during construction. The house frame, having been pre-fabricated, might have been found to entirely fill the width of the site, leaving no space for the chimney stack. Mr Paycocke might have been unable or unwilling to acquire more land.

A major rethink would have been necessary resulting in the fireplace wall being repositioned as an internal partition. This would have reduced the hall and upper chamber to only two bays with no suitable place for a chimney stack.

A ground floor fireplace would have been possible in the rear wall of the western bay and this would not have needed a chimney stack as smoke would have gone out of the old open hall roof. The authentic looking mantel beam now in the parlour could have served the same purpose in the western bay originally.

Possibly the eastern bay (extension) was included within the living accommodation at this point, rather than serving as a detached office.

Mr Thomas Paycocke may have been a less than happy man!

'Intended' dwelling, see plans opposite

0 1   10ft

0   1   3m

Thomas Paycockes 'intended' dwelling

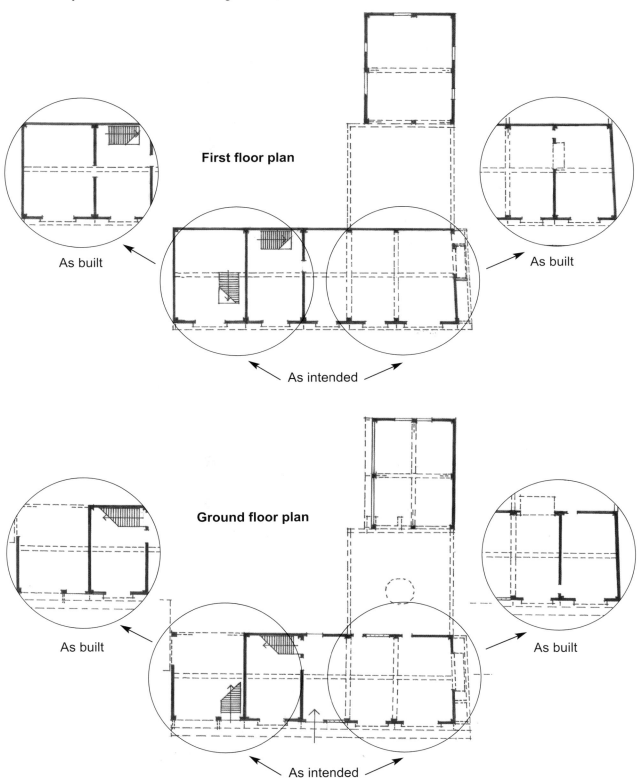

First floor plan

As built

As intended

As built

Ground floor plan

As built

As intended

As built

27 West Street (The Fleece Public House)

A two-and-a-half storey long-wall jetty house of the early 17th century. There is a low attic storey which was clearly influenced by the similar, earlier, attic loft which originally existed at the adjoining Paycocke's House. The building is of six bays, with jowled posts and straight, upwardly angled, primary braces. The plan form is 'traditional' with a cross-passage and service rooms at the western end. There were rear wall fireplaces to hall and parlour. An old photograph shows that one of these had three octagonal flues. The building presents an interesting blend of old and new concepts.

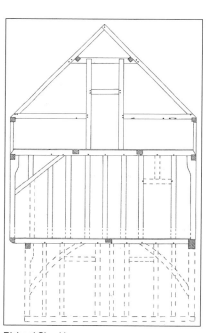

Richard Shackle

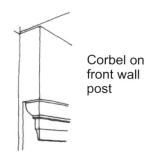

Corbel on front wall post

Section drawing of service wall

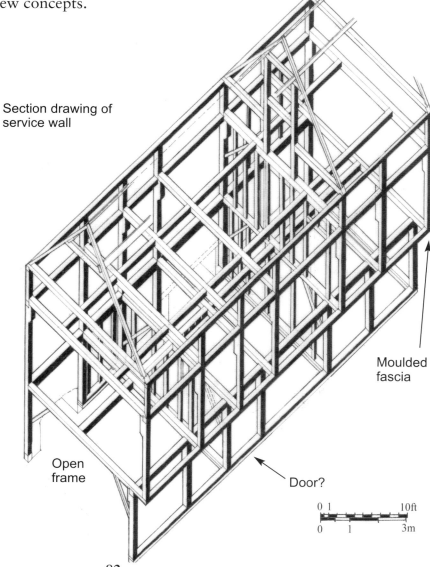

Moulded fascia

Open frame

Door?

0 1   10ft

0   1   3m

31 - 33 - 35 West Street

A handed semi-detached pair of
extremely small, single-ended, in-line
houses, which are notable for the
exposed framing on the front with the
two hall windows having very deep
moulded mullions and trefoil-arched
heads. These heads seem to be
replacements but good copies. The
houses are likely to be a speculative pair
of the mid 15th century. Elaborate
windows in such modest buildings may
have been to attract tenants. There
seems to have been spere
walls to define cross-passages.

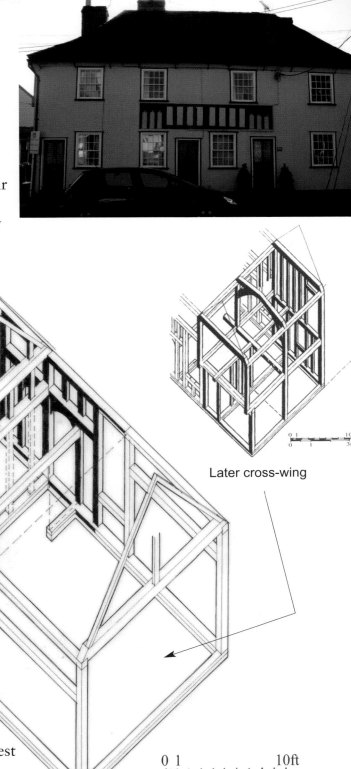

Later cross-wing

At some time in the
16th century, the 'ends'
were partly removed and
replaced with two storey, jettied
cross-wings. It seems probable that
these incorporated high-end recesses.
This pair probably represent the smallest
true domestic units yet recognised in
Coggeshall.

37 West Street

The site dimensions suggest that there were originally four little in-line houses here forming a terrace (including nos. 33-35), or two slightly detached pairs. All that remains is traces of an open hall at 37, together with an unjettied 16th century cross-wing that must have replaced the western unit. This cross-wing has two rooms on each floor and a hip at the rear. The remains of its crown-post roof suggest a post-1550 date. The ground floor front room (parlour) has a little window facing east, to view down the street. A terrace of modest units, in this location, makes sense in being at the very edge of the town.

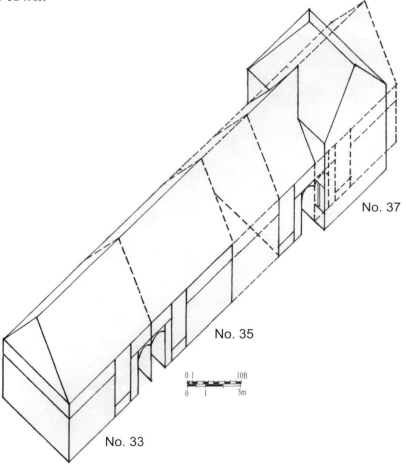

No. 37

No. 35

No. 33

0 1   10ft

0   1   3m

WEST STREET - NORTH SIDE

20 West Street

A jettied, two storey, mid 17th century building of
two unequal bays. The projecting ends of the jettied
bridging joists are elaborately shaped and moulded.
There appears to be second-hand timber, and this,
together with an arbitrary degree of pegging, makes
interpretation difficult. As is typical at this date, the
attic is a contemporary feature. There may have been
a shop in the smaller bay. The front may
have had an applied, moulded, fascia.

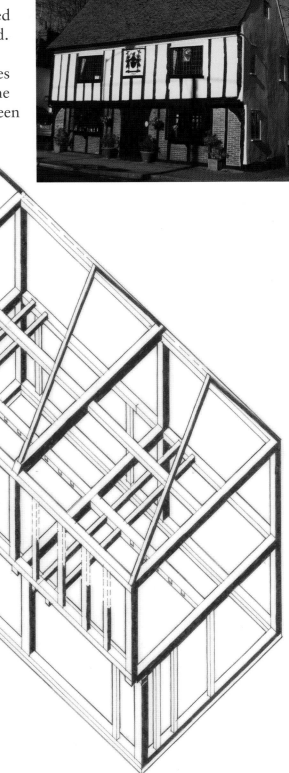

Planted fascia

Moulded jetty

0 1   10ft
0   1   3m

14 West Street

An elegant truss is the best preserved feature of this much altered and extended cross-wing like building. It seems probable that the south bay extended further forward and contained a shop.

There is evidence for a kind of undershot cross-passage leading to a 'half-arched' door which probably opened into one rear room. The floor joists are irregularly spaced (to look impressive from the exterior?). The floor framing in the rear bay looks like a later build.

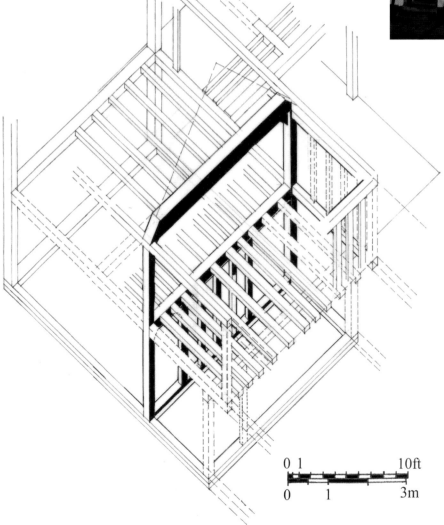

0 1   10ft

0   1   3m

86

12 West Street

A few timbers survive of what was probably a 17th century structure.

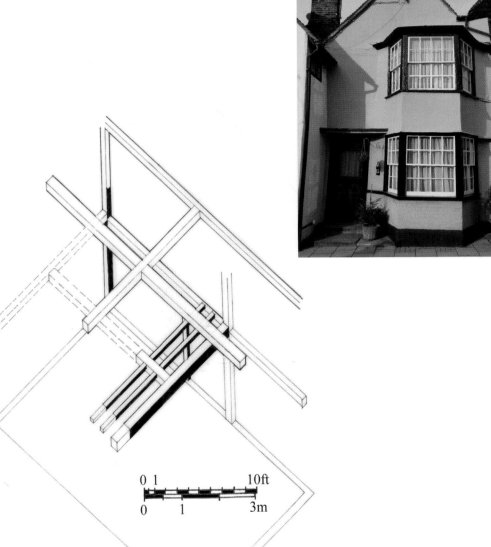

0 1   10ft

0   1   3m

6 - 8 West Street

This seemingly 15th century building has been transformed by an 18th century remodelling. Earlier renovation revealed a moulded bridging joist and moulded floor joists of 15th century character. According to the 1575 survey there wasn't a building on this site. It is likely that this floor has been reused and moved from a structure elsewhere. It is noticeable that reused, moulded joists are relatively common, suggesting that they were too attractive to throw away!

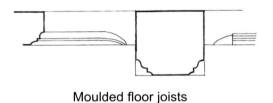

Moulded floor joists

Rear of 6 - 8 West Street

A small two storey building which is similar to, but slightly larger than, the booth stalls described elsewhere in the town. It has no stair trap and was jettied to the west. It was evidently open-framed to a pre-existing structure to the south.

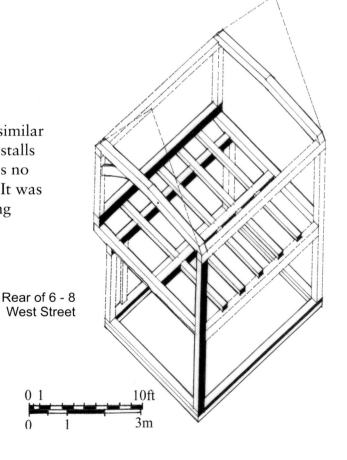

Rear of 6 - 8
West Street

0 1   10ft

0   1   3m

4 West Street

This is a two storey row building, jettied to both frontages. It is of two unequal bays and of extremely fine 15th century carpentry. The roof form is a little uncertain and may have been re-built. There are the remains of a fully arched shop front on the western flank, and possibly one to the south. To the rear first floor there is a door opening with an arched head. The door jamb of this arched opening has wedge shaped fixing mortices, as at the hall windows of Baumanns Restaurant, Stoneham Street.

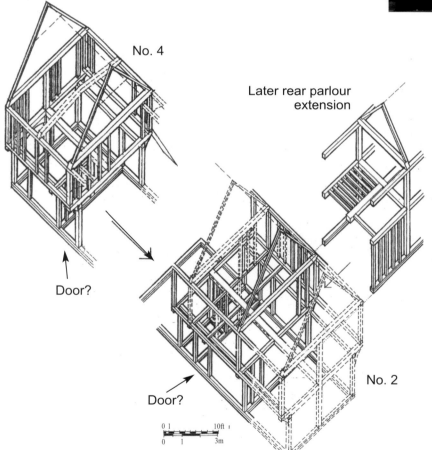

No. 4

Door?

Door?

Later rear parlour extension

No. 2

The associated hall, on site of no. 2, probably was of 'Wealden' form with roof overhangs at front and rear. The presumed external stair case (see page 90) was later replaced by an internal stair trap immediately within the building. These row buildings seem to have stopped at no. 4, with a gap between them and nos. 6 - 8

4 - 2 West Street continued

4 - 2 West Street continued

This sequence shows that nos. 2 and 4 were subject to a rapid series of changes.

Phase 1

Phase 2

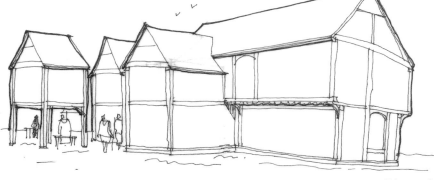

Phase 3

2 West Street

The previous 'Wealden' hall was soon rebuilt in long-wall jetty form with a 'high-end' bay to the east. The latter was then demolished and replaced by the booth/stall at 10 Market End. Later an extra bay was added to the rear (north) which includes a reused floor of moulded joists.

The West Street walk finishes at no. 2

STONEHAM STREET

**The walk begins on the west side of Stoneham Street and returns on the east side.
The southern end of Stoneham Street is called Market Hill**

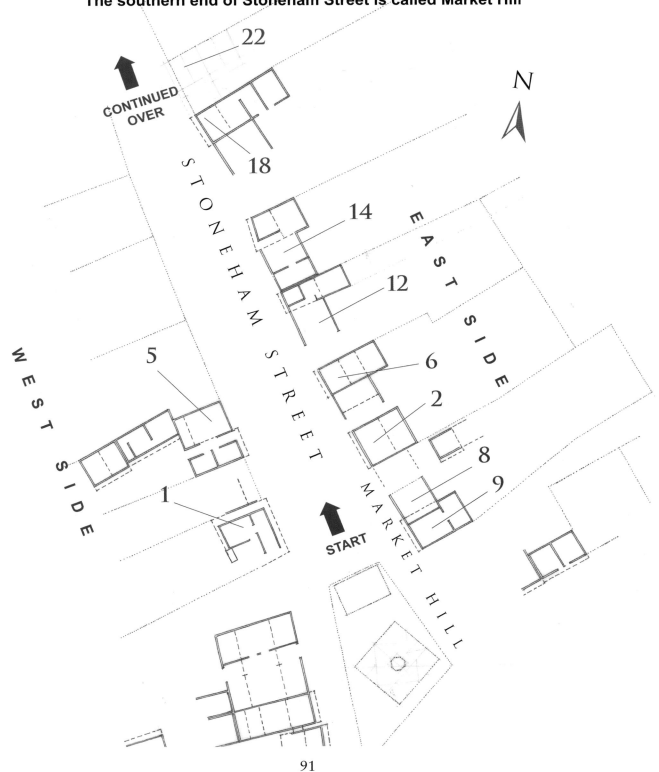

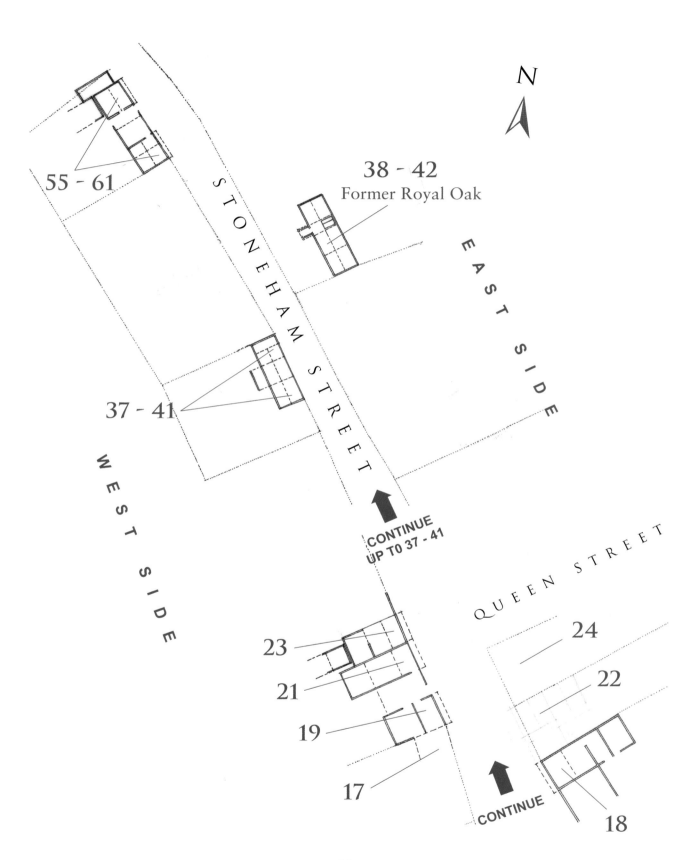

STONEHAM STREET - WEST SIDE

1 Stoneham Street

This is a late 16th century (c.1600?) building of two storeys, jettied to the rear where the jetty extends to carry a pentice. Here there is a domestic hall of two unequal bays and part of another room, with a contemporary stack. The rear oriel window with its frieze windows is particularly impressive. On the Stoneham Street side (east), there is a two storey jettied building, probably a shop. On the north flank are remnants of a much earlier cross-wing. On the south eastern corner is the famous Coggeshall clock tower, which included a four-centred arch within its structure.

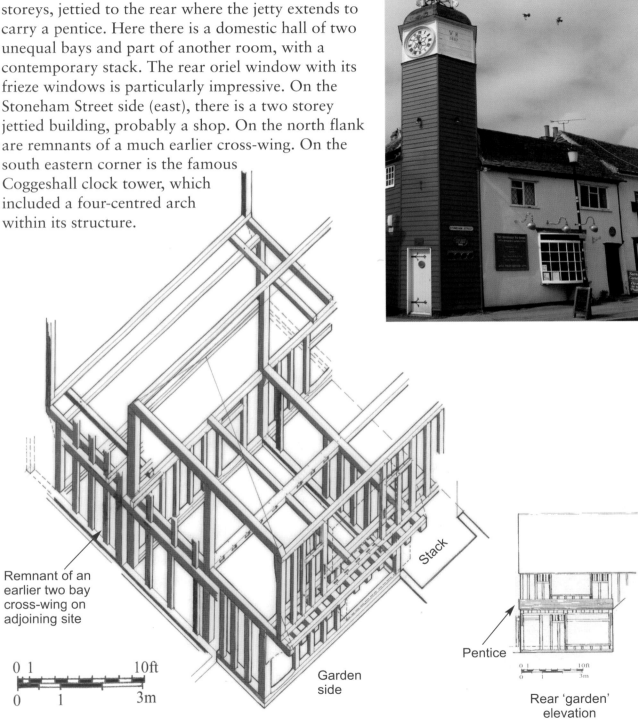

Remnant of an earlier two bay cross-wing on adjoining site

Stack

Garden side

0 1   10ft

0   1   3m

Pentice

0 1   10ft
0   1   3m

Rear 'garden' elevation

5 Stoneham Street

A two storey cross-wing of two slightly unequal bays and an undershot cross-passage. A jettied, later, range to the rear was probably the solar/parlour and has provision for a garderobe at its western end. Beyond this is a further two bay extension that is probably in situ, rather than moved from elsewhere. The cross-wing is likely to be early 15th century, and the rest a series of different builds. In the 16th century the hall was floored with moulded joists and a second gable to the street frontage superimposed on the hall (as at 8 East Street).

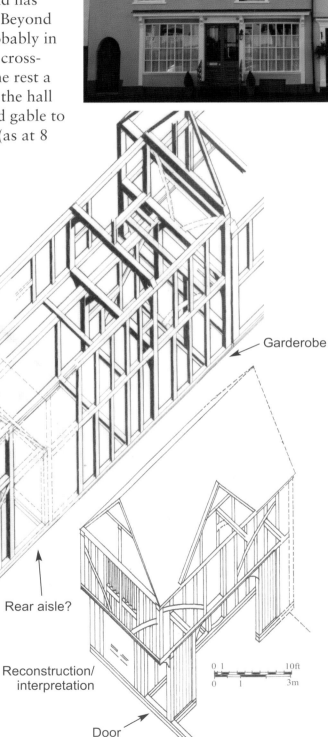

Garderobe

Rear aisle?

Reconstruction/
interpretation

Door

0 1   10ft
0   1   3m

0 1   10ft
0   1   3m

17 Stoneham Street

A tiny fragment of a cross-wing, strangely sited, at right angles, and set a little back from the Stoneham Street frontage. Probably not moved from elsewhere, it has a window opening, shutter groove and an external brace. One can imagine a variety of interpretations!

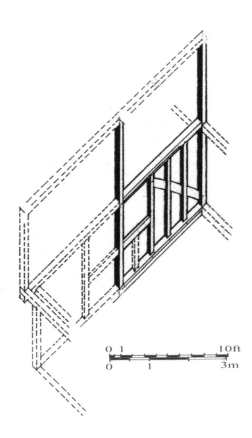

Stoneham Street

19 - 21 Stoneham Street

This is a complete H-plan house with a remarkably small hall. The three bay wing contained parlour/solar and a doorway on the flank leading to a possible external stair. It is conceivable that there might have been a rear aisle and there is a modern flat-roofed room where one would have been sited. The roof form also presents difficulties: it has been rebuilt, but there is a vague possibility that it was of 'Wealden' construction. The southern cross-wing was open-framed on its south flank where there must have been a pre-existing low building.

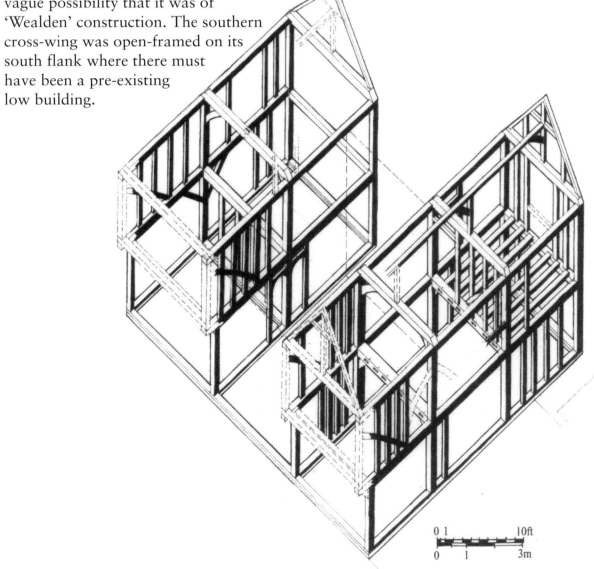

23 Stoneham Street

A cross-wing of three fairly equal bays of c.1560, it is likely to be a high-end wing, with the now demolished hall to the north. The joists have edge rolls and there was a large oriel window on the front gable. The construction of this wing blocked a flank window on the adjoining no. 21. The gap in the cross-partition, between the middle and rear bay, probably housed a brick stack, with fireplaces to parlour and solar. To the rear is part of a small 15th century cross-wing, the siting of which make no real sense. It was probably moved here from another location as a kitchen or outbuilding.

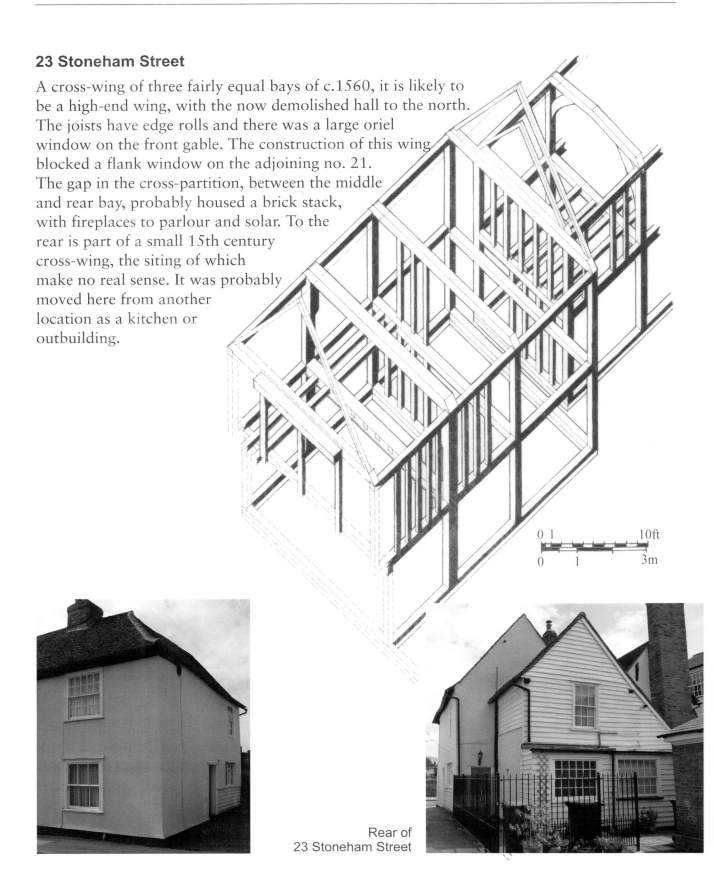

Rear of
23 Stoneham Street

37, 39, 41 Stoneham Street

Now three houses, this 17th century structure was probably built as a workshop or warehouse, with a possible staircase in the short north bay. It has primary bracing, with studs mostly pegged and some seemingly second-hand timber. There are face-halved and bladed scarf-joints and chamfers with lambs-tongue stops. No. 39 has a rear outshot (later?) and this may have continued along the rear.

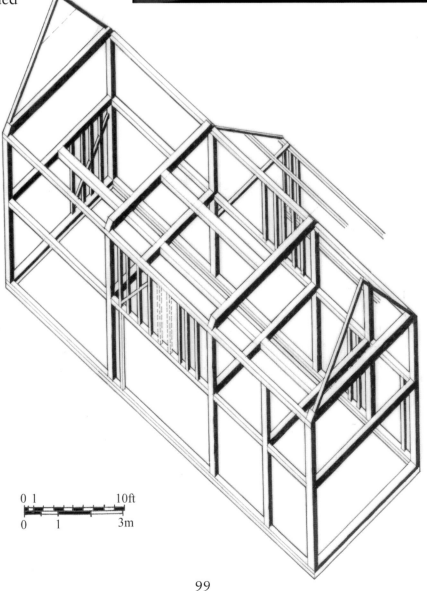

0 1   10ft
0   1   3m

55 - 61 Stoneham Street

This building is difficult to survey, having been divided into five small units, each with an intruding chimneystack. The rental survey of 1575 does not mention any building at this site and records that the rent of the land was only one penny. However, the two cross-wings have been tree-ring dated to 1555, so these structures may have been removed from elsewhere and the long-wall jetty building assembled on the site after 1575. The curious construction with reversed assembly would substantiate this theory.

Under the eaves of the frontage at the southern end is a moulded fascia of late 16th-century character. No. 61 may have been a separate unit and has a timber-framed lean-to on its northern flank which may have been service rooms.

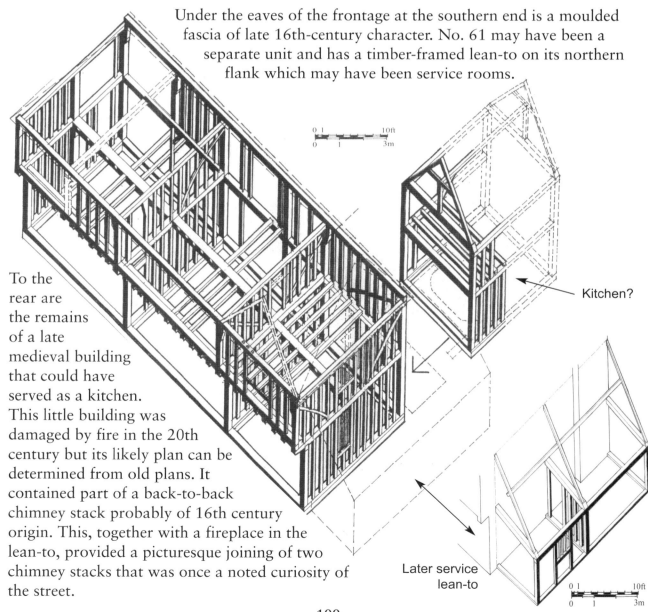

Kitchen?

Later service lean-to

To the rear are the remains of a late medieval building that could have served as a kitchen. This little building was damaged by fire in the 20th century but its likely plan can be determined from old plans. It contained part of a back-to-back chimney stack probably of 16th century origin. This, together with a fireplace in the lean-to, provided a picturesque joining of two chimney stacks that was once a noted curiosity of the street.

STONEHAM STREET - EAST SIDE

38 - 42 Stoneham Street (The Royal Oak)

A mid 17th century two storey house of four bays and of the lobby entry type. The frame is thoroughly pegged together and there are slightly curved primary braces. Surprisingly, there was no structural partition between the hall and the southern bay, but this was rectified later (see Hutleys, Church Street). The stack has mantle beams to both faces. The stairs in front of the stack are contemporary and typical of the period. Contemporary, or near contemporary, jettied porch, and gabled roof extension (late 17th century?) to extend the staircase to the attics.

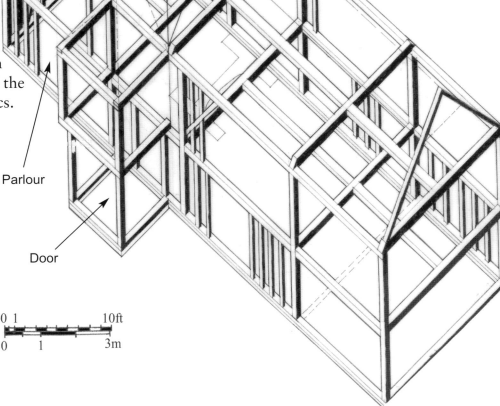

Parlour

Door

0 1   10ft

0   1   3m

24 Stoneham Street (Weavers Cottage)

This sketch is based largely on the statutory list description. It is a 16th century in-line house of two unequal bays with jowled posts. There is a stair hole against the partition in the south bay. The south end is open framed against no. 22.

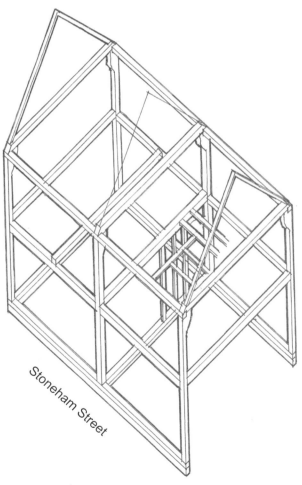

22 Stoneham Street (Olde Stoneham)

Unfortunately, this building has been only approximately measured. Of the 15th century, it has a four bay, jettied cross-wing and remarkably small hall. The exact size of this hall depends on whether it abutted directly on to 18, or whether there was a small gap (where there is now a through passage). The cross-wing involves the most logical 'urban' solution, with the two service rooms, behind a two bay parlour. There may have been a flank lean-to (as at the Through Inn, East Street) so as to be able to reach these service rooms, in the dry. A very similar solution exists at Horn Farm, Salcot, in Essex. This seems to be one of the clearer examples of a door in a cross-wing flank, leading to a seeming platform and stairs down into the hall. There are suggestions of a similar arrangement in other Coggeshall buildings and this would seem an odd idea to make best use of limited space. The platform, or 'gallery' can only be glimpsed via the mysterious, horizontal timbers, in The Chapel Inn. No. 22 was eventually reconstructed as a long-wall jetty house and this tended to confuse the issues.

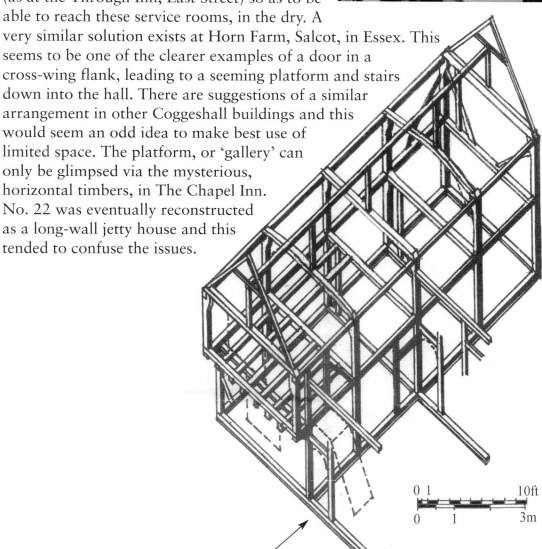

Door

0 1   10ft
0   1   3m

Stoneham Street, east side looking south

18 Stoneham Street

An unusual 15th century four bay cross-wing with the front two bays functioning as a parlour. The large flank opening framed a staircase that was partly outside of the main frame. A similar staircase in a fairly similar cross-wing exists at the Council Offices, 17 South Street, Rochford, Essex. The rear bay has a central storey post, for no apparent reason (see also 10 East Street) and a contemporary attic floor, a remarkably early example. There is a hole in the framing of the north flank for some indeterminate type of early chimney stack, probably to heat both the parlour and the solar over it. The part-inside, part-outside staircase at 18 Stoneham Street is possibly a woollen trade feature.The only other known example is at 17 South Street, Rochford, where the cross-wing is of a similar design.

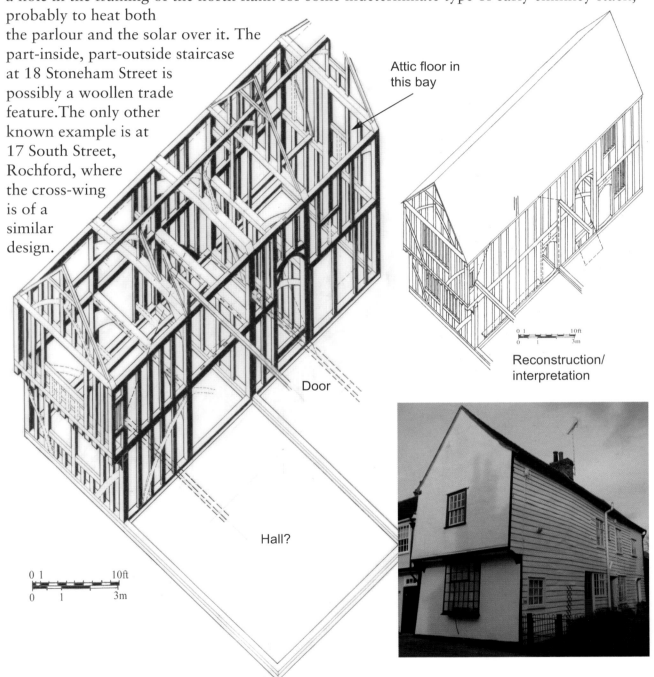

Attic floor in this bay

Door

Hall?

Reconstruction/ interpretation

14 Stoneham Street

A 15th century two bay cross-wing, with undershot cross-passage leading to the rear bay. The hall has been demolished, its height can be determined from existing mortices in the side of the cross-wing. At the south end is an in-line parlour/chamber bay with a central door to the parlour (as at Spooners, Church Street).

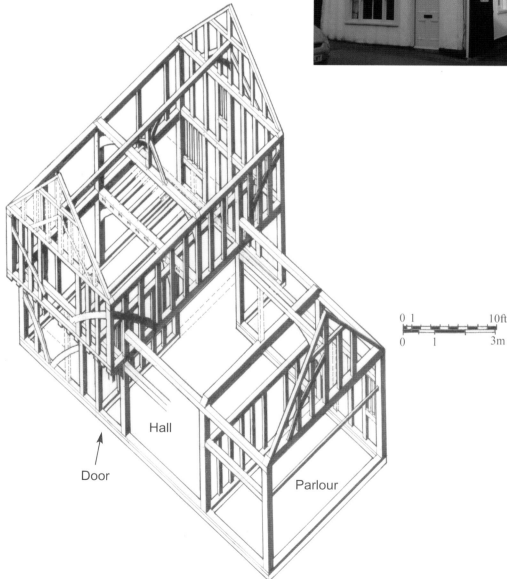

Hall

Door

Parlour

0 1   10ft

0   1   3m

12 Stoneham Street

This is a 15th century cross-wing of three bays, probably a 'single ender'. There was a high end recess for the owner's bench, and a relatively low hall. As is often the case, it is now impossible to detect evidence for a staircase. The rear bay at the first floor seems to have been a substantial separate chamber. The position of the former hall now contains a two storey 17th century structure of unremarkable character.

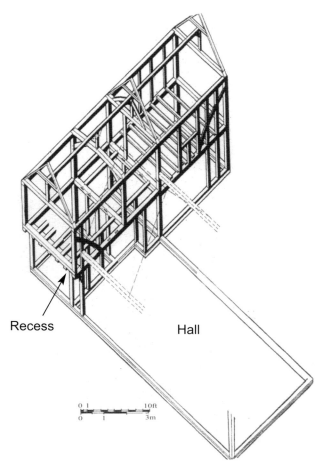

Recess   Hall

0 1   10ft
0   1   3m

6 - 2 Stoneham Street

This appears to be an H-plan house although it is now impossible to detect any physical linkage between the open-hall and the southern cross-wing. The hall is of two unequal bays with a splendid octagonal crown post with a moulded capital. Traces of the rear hall window have wedge shaped recesses in the jambs, like the door opening in no. 4 Market Hill. There is a good example of a three bay solar in the north wing, which appears to be at the low end of the hall.

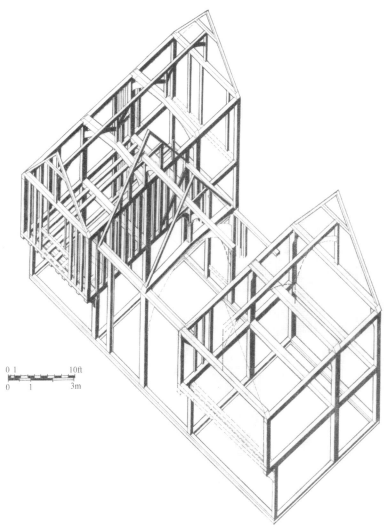

7 - 8 Market Hill

The frontage has a minimal two storey structure of seemingly late date and a timber with passing-brace halvings reused as a tie-beam. To the rear is a curious little jettied building, resembling a market booth-stall which was open framed against a lost building.

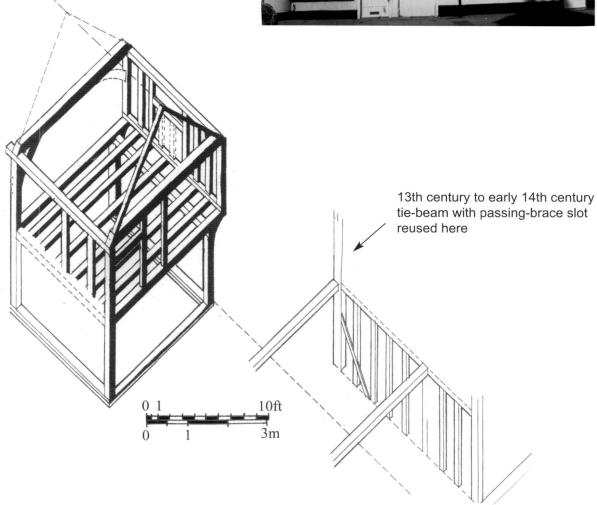

13th century to early 14th century tie-beam with passing-brace slot reused here

0 1   10ft
0   1   3m

9 Market Hill

This early cross-wing is difficult to measure because of the usual interior fittings of a shop. It seems relatively early (note the big braces to upper tie-beams) and there was a probable high end recess on the northern flank. There are two possible door openings to the rear ground floor room with shutter like grooves over their heads. Were there 'shutter doors' slid up from the bottom?

The wall with the high-end recess has been so severely rebuilt that it seems to shuffle the unconnected elements. Probably, the current upper wall framing, was originally the ground floor wall with the ogee-headed door opening originally leading to the parlour. Such a limited width recess can be seen at Myddylton Place in Saffron Walden.

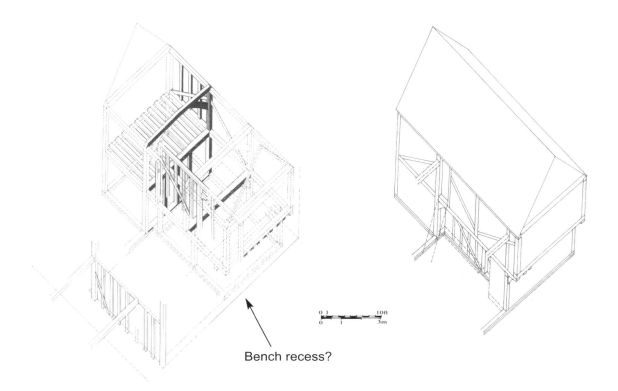

Bench recess?

The Stoneham Street walk finishes at 9 Market Hill

THE 'MARKET HOUSES', CENTRE OF THE MARKET PLACE

In 1499-1500, Thomas Halle of Coksale bequeathed the funding for a chapel with a little garden. This was situated 'opposite' the Chapel Inn in the middle of the Market Place. Whether this building was of masonry, or timber-framing, is now unknown. By 1588, the Chapel had been re-used as the corn market house, when it was granted to certain citizens of Coggeshall. These persons, who were fullers and weavers, then converted the old chapel into a market house, with meeting room and storage. A stone building might

Market area looking east

have been easier to convert, by building an upper floor. The new structure contained a bell, to summon apprentices to work, and a clock. It was obviously two-storey, and a poor weaver or comber was employed to clean the market house underneath, receiving a fee from traders who used the space. It would seem from this that there was a partly open area underneath and stairs up to the first floor. One of the later occupants was referred to as crier and market clerk. From 1635 till 1719 the property is referred to as the Corn and Butter Market Houses (plural). In 1774 it was known as the Market Houses.

When the building was pulled down in 1787, the clock and bell were set up in the octagonal tower on the west side of Stoneham Street. It seems probable that this clock and bell were originally enclosed in a similar octagonal turret on the roof of the 1588 building. Other mentions of this building, or buildings, refer to a 'cloth hall' and this was probably a

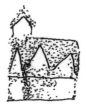

first floor space, like that that still survives in Stockwell, Colchester. The building is represented as having two or three gables, a turret, and possibly a jetty on a map of 1731, and as a tiny black square on the Chapman and André map of 1777. When this structure stood, it must have been an eye-catching feature in the middle of the town.

View of 'Market Houses' from 18th century map

The general location of the chapel, garden and market house was recorded in the 19th century as the space had been defined by a series of wooden posts. This roughly triangular area is shown on page 113, but the building shapes are conjectural. This largish area could have contained one or more buildings and had probably gained, through continuing use, other ancillary market place features.

111

The walk begins on the north side of Market End at Doubleday Corner, outside the Co-op, and proceeds in a anti-clockwise direction

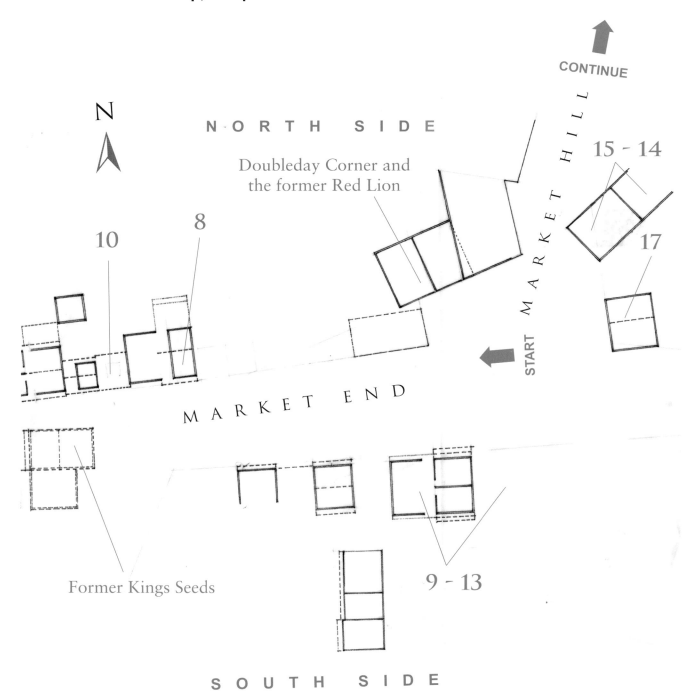

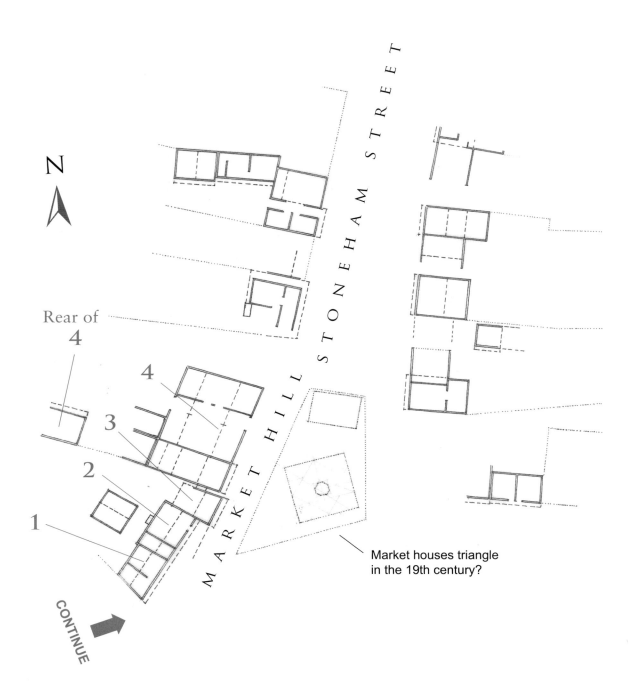

N

Rear of
4

4

3

2

1

M A R K E T   H I L L

S T O N E H A M   S T R E E T

Market houses triangle
in the 19th century?

CONTINUE

MARKET END NORTH

Doubleday Corner and the former Red Lion Public House

In 1896 the Red Lion was seriously damaged by fire and subsequently demolished. The adjacent drawing is based on contemporary photographs, although they do not present an overall panorama. The Red Lion was at a curious angle to the street. Its diagonal set-back is more or less perpetuated by the present 1960s block of shops (which include the Co-op). Its position may indicate an older frontage line which has been encroached upon elsewhere and which was determined by the presence of the stream originating in Church Street.

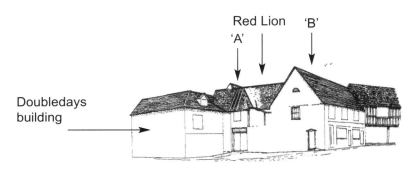

Part 'A' above was clearly a late medieval building, with a crown-post roof. Block 'B', to the right, was a more substantial range with an impressive gable end. This, from the evidence of the pictures, looks later and possibly 17th century.

The former Doubledays, also long demolished, could well have been a late medieval cross-wing that marked the beginning of a former market row. A building is documented on the Doubledays site from the 13th century.

The 1575 survey notes a pair of market stalls west of the former Doubledays building.

Market End view of booth/stalll

8 Market End

The first surviving building in a 'market row', this two storey structure has also suffered fires, apparently on more than one occasion. There are two remaining bays, with a jetty to the south and an undershot cross-passage. The floor joists in the rear bay are placed at right angles to those in the front. This probably means that there was originally a third jettied bay, projecting to the rear. (This reversing of the floor must have had an advantage and extra third bays have been noted elsewhere). The structure would then be a cross-wing, probably containing a shop in the front. To the west there was probably a small open-hall, but this area has been completely rebuilt. It is possible that the postulated rear third bay was accessed from the undershot cross-passage (see no. 14 West Street).

Whilst this 'Market Row' may well have functioned as such, as witnessed by the presence of jetties on its northern side, the land to the 'rear' of the building probably remained private. This would explain why this northern side never became public highway and allowed gardens and extensions to eventually appear.

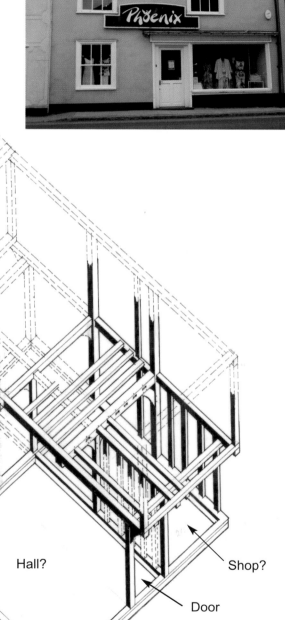

Hall?

Shop?

Door

0 1   10ft

0   1   3m

10 Market End

This, much extended house contains two tiny timber structures on the Market End frontage. The western one of these was a permanent market stall of the 'booth' type and was jettied front and rear. There are the remains of a undershot cross-passage and a stair trap to the little chamber above. The eastern unit appears to have been similar but only remnants survive. Within the rear of no. 10 is another, square, two storey box, without a jetty, with the upper floor probably gained via an external ladder. This was probably a further booth stall of somewhat more utilitarian design.

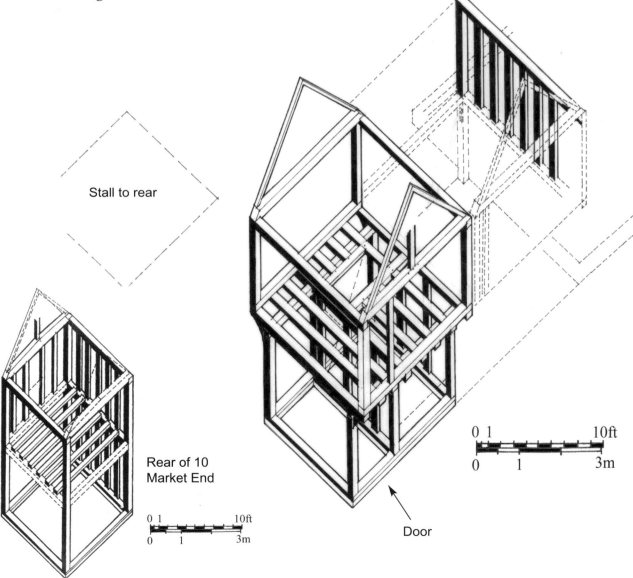

Stall to rear

Rear of 10
Market End

Door

0 1   10ft
0   1   3m

0 1   10ft
0   1   3m

MARKET END SOUTH

Former Kings Seeds

This view is based on an old photograph as the building was demolished in the last century. It appears to have been a two storey cross-wing with a hipped rear roof and gable. Some old views show the remains of an attached hall roof to the south. A peep view is further provided of a two storey range beyond, that has all disappeared and was probably a 17th century timber framed building (workshop?).

There was probably a row of market stalls between this King's building and the flank of the former Cricketers.

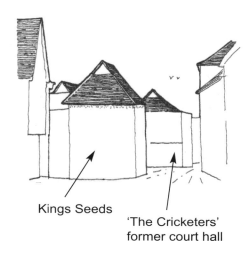

Kings Seeds

'The Cricketers' former court hall

9 - 13 Market End (Cavendish House and the White Hart)

This impressive house stands on tip-toe on a relatively small site, in a key position in the town. It comprises a single bay hall and a three-storey cross-wing that was jettied on each floor at front and rear. The hall, at about 320 square feet, had a boarded spere wall (not drawn) with octagonal posts and a moulded head rail, fragments of which survive in the rear wall. The roof is

of queen post construction. A square trimmed hole astride the roof has cut-outs suggesting a former octagonal smoke louvre, such as survives more completely at the nearby Chapel Inn.

As a vernacular form, queen post roofs flourished in central East Anglia as an alternative to the more usual crown posts. This roof type derives from the 'raised aisle' hall concept, which has a similar geographical distribution, with outliers in Hertfordshire and Essex. Here the roof is elaborated in a manner akin to a raised aisle example, with square set purlins and octagonal posts. Some of the detail is reminiscent of The Stables at Fressingfield, Suffolk.

9 - 13 Market End continued

9 - 13 Market End (Cavendish House and the White Hart) continued

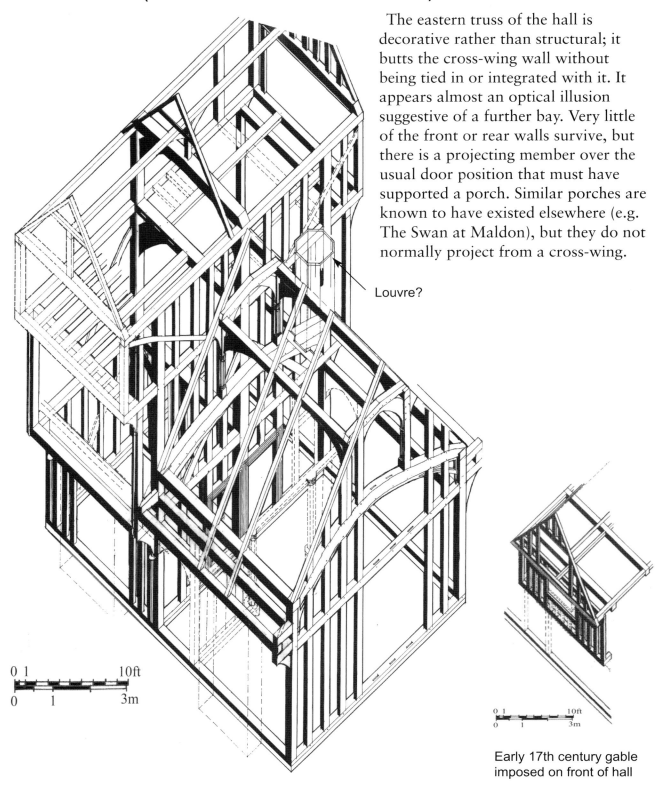

The eastern truss of the hall is decorative rather than structural; it butts the cross-wing wall without being tied in or integrated with it. It appears almost an optical illusion suggestive of a further bay. Very little of the front or rear walls survive, but there is a projecting member over the usual door position that must have supported a porch. Similar porches are known to have existed elsewhere (e.g. The Swan at Maldon), but they do not normally project from a cross-wing.

Louvre?

0 1   10ft
0   1   3m

0 1   10ft
0   1   3m

Early 17th century gable imposed on front of hall

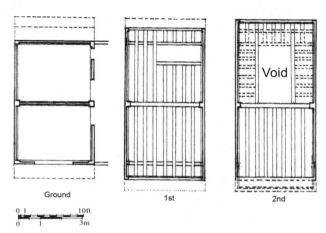

Ground

0 1   10ft
0   1   3m

Floor plans of no. 9 Market End (Cavendish House)

1st

Void

2nd

The two doors in the side of the cross-wing have unusually elaborate surrounds. The ground floor of the cross-wing most likely consisted of service rooms. The front elevation had a pair of studs either side of a wide opening. On balance, this seems unlikely to have been a shop front as was no alternative location for a service room. The first floor of the cross-wing would have provided a largish solar. There is a hint of a window in the east wall at this level.

In the late 16th century a floor was inserted into the open hall, which also gained a display gable added to the front roof pitch, a typical detail for Coggeshall at this period.

The unusual quality and design of this building can be attributed to the employment of a non-local carpenter, probably from north of the Essex border.

Grotesque face on jetty bracket
of Cavendish House

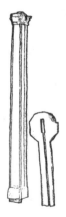

Remains of spere truss from Greensted - similar
to that formerly in the White Hart

119

MARKET END EAST

17 Market Hill

Two-storey building probably of two equal bays, without a jetty. The southern wall is now canted and this may be an alteration to effectively widen East Street. The ground floor has three, or possibly four, diamond mullion windows. The upper floor has been reduced in height and then raised again in later framing (fire damage?). There is the suggestion of a door opening in the eastern flank and this remnant of a building is clearly incomplete. A timber on the north side may be a relic of a structure (stall?) on that side.

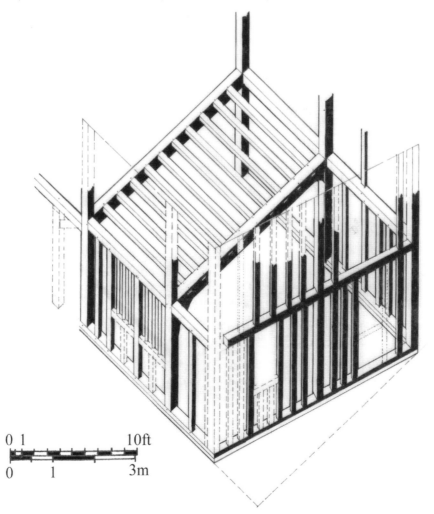

0 1   10ft

0   1   3m

14/15 Market Hill

This early 17th century building, which may have been of two phases, seems to stand over the Church Street stream. This may account for the extremely low ground floor and the upper floor is extremely tall. The south western corner is now canted, but was probably square and the result of an early street widening. This corner block was probably three storied and the upper part has been damaged by fire. The main body of the building has a remarkably steep roof.

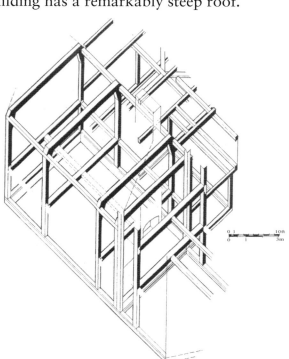

Rear of 14/15 Market End

This small building is jettied on three sides and backed on to the Church Street stream. It looks 15th century, but is in fact early 17th century making use of some earlier framing.

The adjoining jettied range is early 17th century and clearly an extension to the Market End frontage building. All of this provides a picturesque group, now largely concealed in a tucked away courtyard.

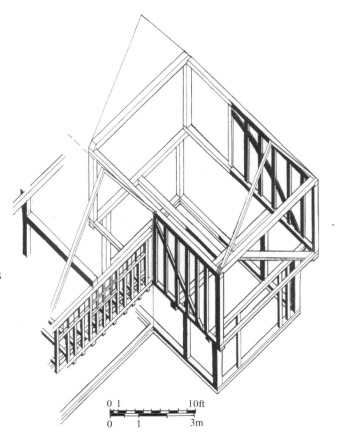

The Chapel Inn, 4 Market Hill

The Chapel Inn is probably the largest and most significant early house in the town. It probably existed at the time of the of the Peasants Revolt in 1381, being identifiable with the property belonging to John Sewell, sheriff of Essex, which was attacked by the rebels. It has proved a difficult building to measure as much is obscured and altered. The hall is of three bays with a spere truss and probably a base cruck truss, and aisles to both front and rear.

The southern high end cross-wing is of three bays with a three-bay parlour and solar of two bays. The narrow sub-bay to the rear possibly contained a staircase.

The above drawing shows, in dotted line, aisles that would be generated by extending the steep pitch of the hall roof. It is more likely that the aisles were wider, with a slacker pitch than the main roof. There was an in-line 'end' to the north, now largely demolished, but surviving in part in the adjoining building.

The roof has the base structure of an octagonal smoke louvre, but it has proved impossible to measure its precise position. The north flank of the cross-wing has bracing in a simple East Anglian 'fan pattern' and there are splayed scarf joints with under-squinted abutments. To the rear (west) of the cross-wing is a probable kitchen extension, still used for this purpose. Adjoining this is another two storey, probably 16th century, block. A floor was introduced over the hall in the 17th century.

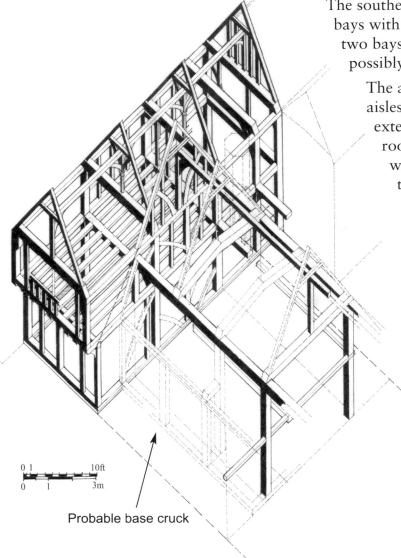

0 1   10ft
0   1   3m

Probable base cruck

Rear of Chapel Inn, 4 Market Hill

This is likely to be the building described as a 'barn' in the 1575 rental survey. It is of three regular bays forming one large first floor chamber. Of early to mid 16th century date, it was open-framed against a low building to the west. The ground floor looks somewhat more utilitarian with a curious arrangement of external openings. It may have been used by a clothier as a wool-house or woolhall, probably serving the Chapel Inn. In more recent times it was certainly used for stabling in association with the inn.

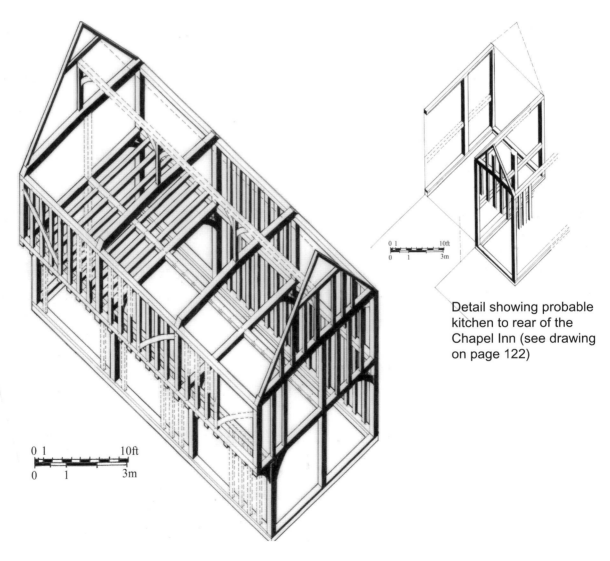

0 1   10ft
0   1   3m

0 1   10ft
0   1   3m

Detail showing probable kitchen to rear of the Chapel Inn (see drawing on page 122)

3 Market Hill

This is a much rebuilt cross-wing that survives as a flank wall and a series of re-sited floor joists. No. 3, with its former hall, must have projected slightly forward of the present frontage line. The cross-wing was probably of three bays but is now dramatically truncated. An early rubble and tile built chimney stack can be seen on the north-east flank which belonged to the Chapel Inn.

3 Market Hill

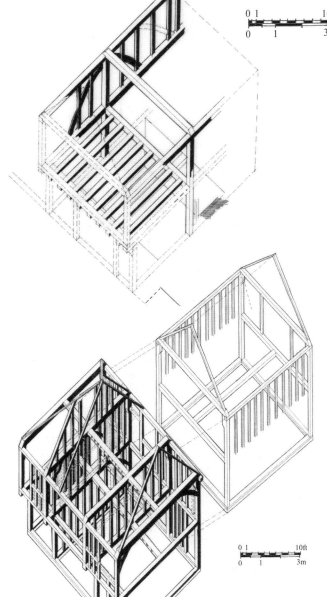

2 Market Hill

2 Market Hill

This building also has mid-rails, and is of similar, but not identical, carpentry to no. 1. Originally it had a hipped roof to the south-west, and was open-framed against the pre-existing no. 3. The small room on the ground floor could have been a shop. There is evidence for a rear wall chimney stack, heating the upper floor at least. To the rear is a lightly framed extension which was elaborately remodelled in the 18th century, with a particularly attractive brick west wall. The position of former attic dormers in the front block can be determined by the design of the floor.

1 Market Hill

An early 17th century jettied two storey building of two unequal bays, it is open-framed to the south east, probably against a long demolished Red Lion (see Market End). There are straight braces to the tie-beams, some primary when in partitions. The upper floor (as no. 3) has a mid-rail, virtually unknown in Essex, and an idea probably borrowed from afar.

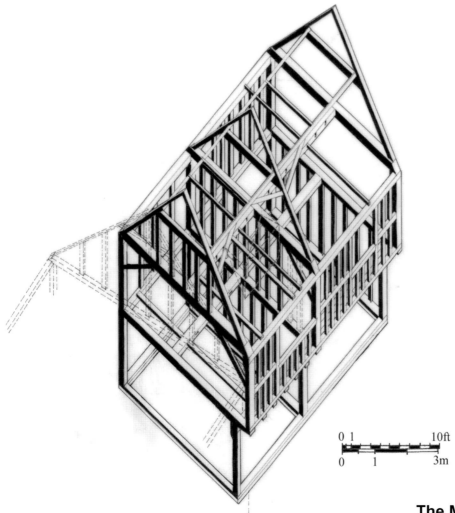

0 1   10ft
0   1   3m

The Market Houses walk finishes at 1 Market Hill

POSTCRIPT

This survey was possible because many old buildings survive in reasonable order. Largely this is because they are enjoyed and cared for by their present day owners. Nevertheless statutory 'listing' and Conservation Area designation, have played a part where this heritage is recognised as being of more than local significance.

I suggest that the attractive 'village urban' character of Coggeshall still has lessons for us today.

The *Essex Design Guide* (1973) attempted to translate these qualities into a framework for modern housing development. Some of its effects can be detected in the post mid 1970s development around the fringes of the old settlement. Such an approach emphasises continuity and a humane and 'people scaled' environment. It is hoped that this study will help us all appreciate the real intellectual effort that underlies our old towns and villages.

David Stenning, former architect and conservation advisor

GLOSSARY

This glossary explains technical terms relating to medieval buildings and timber-framing used in the text. There are at present no accepted national standards for this terminology. The words used here reflect current usage amongst those who study Essex buildings. Some of the words are ancient, but some are convenient labels adopted to describe well recognised features.

Aisled hall: a medieval hall house which has a central hall open to the roof and one or two aisles, usually separated from the hall by arcade posts.

Arch brace: brace rising from a post to an upper horizontal timber, to provide triangulation and strength.

Arched shop front: shop window opening with full arch, usually four-centred.

Bay: spatial units into which a building can be divided, defined by square or rectangular groups of opposed major posts.

Bench: at the high end of an open hall there was usually a bench fixed to the wall for the householder and his family.

Bracing: diagonally set timbers to triangulate and strengthen a wall or open frame, sometimes used decoratively.

Brasier: an iron receptacle which contains burning charcoal to warm a room.

Bressumer: a jetty bressumer is a horizontal timber forming the outer part of a jetty, housing the jointed ends of the projecting floor joists, and generally moulded.

Bridging joist: an internal principal flooring timber linking opposed storey posts.

Butt purlin roof: a roof in which the purlins are pegged into the side of the principal rafters. In Essex such roofs are most typical of the 16th and 17th centuries.

Chamfer: where the otherwise sharp corners of a timber have been cut away, generally to remove the vulnerable sapwood but often for decorative effect.

Clasped purlin roof: a roof in which two longitudinal purlins are supported by collars attached to the rafters about every nine feet. Each collar clasps the purlin in a notch at the outer end of the collar.

Collar: a horizontal timber which ties two rafters together, usually two-thirds of the way up the roof triangle.

Collar purlin: a horizontal longitudinal timber on the centre line of a roof, supported by the crown posts on the tie-beams and itself supporting the collars between the rafter trusses.

Cross-wing: tall, usually jettied, two-storey block with a roof at right angles to the main range.

Crown post roof: a roof with a vertical post at the centre of each tie-beam supporting a collar purlin, to which it is also connected by braces. Sitting on the collar purlin at regular intervals are the collars of the rafter pairs. This type of roof was very popular from about 1250 to 1600 in Essex. Variants are octagonal crown posts, an elaborate form with four-way braces springing from a moulded capital; and cross-quadrate crown posts, which have four attached shafts each running up to and continuous with arched braces.

Diamond mullions: square window mullions set at 45°, the prevalent form of unglazed window opening.

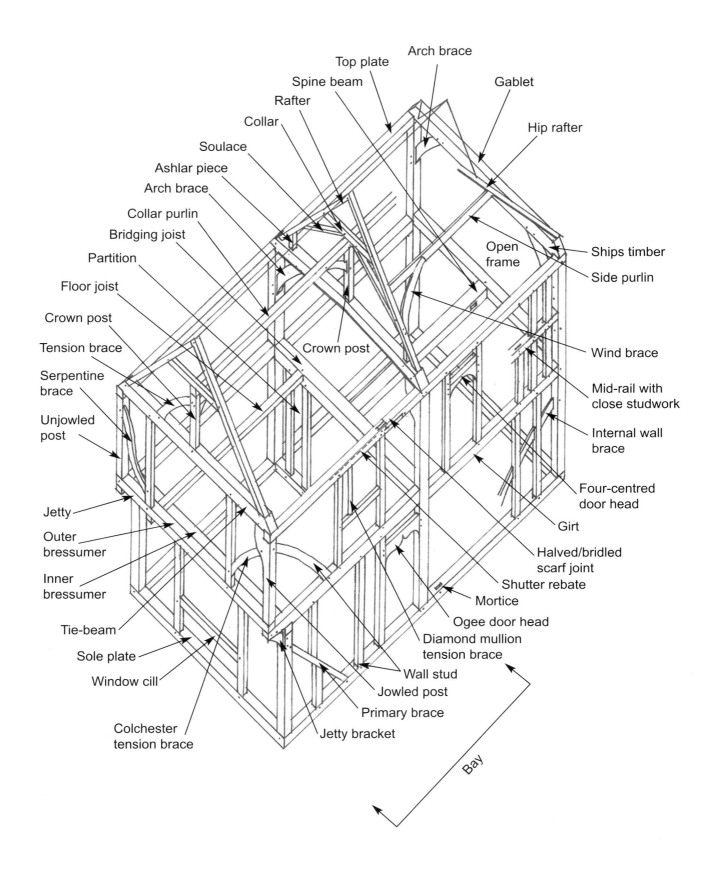

Arch brace

Top plate

Spine beam

Rafter

Collar

Soulace

Ashlar piece

Arch brace

Collar purlin

Bridging joist

Partition

Floor joist

Crown post

Tension brace

Serpentine brace

Unjowled post

Jetty

Outer bressumer

Inner bressumer

Tie-beam

Sole plate

Window cill

Colchester tension brace

Gablet

Hip rafter

Open frame

Ships timber

Side purlin

Crown post

Wind brace

Mid-rail with close studwork

Internal wall brace

Four-centred door head

Girt

Halved/bridled scarf joint

Shutter rebate

Mortice

Ogee door head

Diamond mullion tension brace

Wall stud

Jowled post

Primary brace

Jetty bracket

Bay

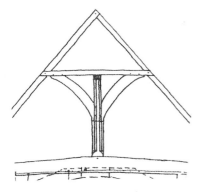

Cross-quadrate crown post with four way bracing, 19 East Street

External brace: brace housed across the wall studs and exposed on the external face of the wall.

Fascia: an applied moulded timber attached to a wall above a jetty, often difficult to distinguish from a jetty bressumer.

Four-centred arch: an arch struck from four compass centres. The usual form of door head in Coggeshall.

Gablet: small gable at the top of a hipped roof, to act as a ventilator or let out smoke. Surprisingly rare in Coggeshall (but see the former Cricketers) though common in Essex.

Garderobe: small rectangular projecting latrine, usually at first floor level at the back of a cross-wing.

Girt: a principal horizontal timber marking a storey height on the exterior of a timber frame.

Half arched shop front: shop window opening strengthened by short curved arched brackets each side.

High end: the end of a hall furthest away from the cross-passage, where the owner of the house sat and dined, reflecting a hierarchical use of space.

High end recess: where the high end bench of the open hall is set back under the parlour which in effect forms a canopy over it, representing an economical use of space in cramped urban conditions.

In-line plan: a simple traditional house plan where there is one single roof, covering the parlour, hall and service end, usually parallel to the street.

Internal brace: brace housed across the face of the studs and exposed on the internal face of the wall. Usually restricted to the 16th century in Essex, but appears earlier in Coggeshall, possibly because the density of the buildings meant that braces were concealed by adjacent structures.

Jetty: where the upper floors of a building project out over the ground floor, the floor joists being supported by and extending beyond the lower jetty beam.

Jetty bracket: curved timber linking a major post with a jettied floor joist.

Joist: common joists are minor intermediate flooring timbers, usually jointed into a spine beam and pegged, or rested on a wall girt or bressumer. Both they and the major bridging joists and spine beams may have chamfered or moulded edges.

Jowled post: a vertical post with a swelling or projection at the top obtained by inverting the tree trunk, making it possible to form a three-way joint between the post, top plate and tie-beam. Posts without jowls are typical of the timber-framing of Colchester, and are also found in Coggeshall, suggesting that the town was at the meeting of two carpentry traditions.

Lobby-entry plan: house plan common from c.1600, in which typically there is a central, or almost central, chimney stack, dividing the ground floor into two rooms, usually a kitchen and a parlour. On one side of the chimney there is the front door and an entrance lobby, and on the other side a winding stair to the first floor.

Long wall jetty house: house with an upper floor over the hall, something typically made possible by the introduction of brick chimneys, and a jetty running along the entire front of the house.

Louvre: a form of smoke outlet on the ridge of the roof, of which there were two octagonal timber ones at Coggeshall.

Low end: the end of the hall adjoining the cross-passage and service rooms.

Mullion: vertical window bar, which may be set diamond-wise, or moulded, commonly from the 16th century with ovolo or quadrant mouldings.

Ogee door head: arched head formed of four inverted curves. Generally a 14th century form, reflecting the Decorated style in masonry architecture.

Oriel window: projecting window, usually with a moulded head and cill.

Pantry: at the low end of a medieval house there were two service rooms, one was the pantry were dry goods such as bread were stored. The other room was the buttery where wet goods were stored.

Parlour: the best downstairs room in a traditional house.

Pegs: large oak pins which hold a medieval building together. Up until the 17th century every stud would be pegged top and bottom. In the 17th century they started pegging every other stud and sometimes even less frequently than that. In many medieval buildings, particularly in the roof, the pegs were allowed to project several inches either side of the joint.

Post: a main vertical timber supporting a building.

Primary brace: a feature of later framing, from the end of the 16th century, in which the brace is the full thickness of the wall and interrupts the studs.

Purlin: a longitudinal timber running below the rafters to strengthen the roof.

Queen post roof: in this type of roof, two posts equally spaced rise up from the tie beam and support square set purlins which are tied together by a collar. At Coggeshall this type of roof only occurs at the White Hart where there is a superb example.

Rafter: one of a pair of inclined timbers that make up a truss forming the triangular shape of the roof. In late medieval Essex buildings, the normal pitch is about 50°.

Scarf joint: a carpenter's joint that joins two timbers end to end horizontally, where the individual timbers would otherwise be too short.

Serpentine brace: double curved braces, sometimes of the mid to late 14th century (Spooners, Church Street), but revived in the late 16th century.

Service rooms: in the traditional medieval house plan, there was a pair of service rooms at the 'low' end of the hall, often referred to as the buttery and pantry for the storage or liquid and dry goods respectively. This arrangement cannot often be recognised at Coggeshall, probably because of the shortage of space in densely built up conditions, and because the service rooms may have become parlours and shops.

Shop: a small room on the ground floor of a building with a shop window opening on to a street. The word can mean either a retail shop or a workshop or both.

Shutter: fitting made of boards to exclude the weather from an unglazed window or shop front.

Shutter groove or rebate: slot or rebate in the soffit of a horizontal timber to house an internal shutter.

Smoke louvre: a structure on the roof of an open hall to let the smoke out.

Solar: the best upstairs room in a traditional house. Sometimes found at the 'low' end because of the constraints of space in an urban context.

Sole plate: a horizontal beam at the base of a wall, into which the studs and posts are tenoned. It usually rests on a plinth wall made of flint, tile or brick.

Spere: two posts or short screens which separate the hall from the cross passage, acting as draught screen.

Spine beam: a principal horizontal timber running down the centre line of a building.

Splayed scarf joint: an early type of scarf joint, mostly restricted to the 13th and 14th centuries, but can be found later, typically in collar purlins

Stair tower: a tower attached to a house containing a staircase, which would be much easier to use than the usual ladder stairs found in medieval houses.

Storey post: major vertical timber which defines the 'bays' of a building.

Studs: vertical intermediate timbers in a wall, the spaces between them filled with wattle and daub or exceptionally brick nogging (in Coggeshall, Paycockes House only).

Tension brace: brace rising from a horizontal timber to a vertical post, the normal walling type in Coggeshall. Braces rising from a vertical timber or stud to a post are a feature, together with posts lacking jowls, of Colchester carpentry.

Tie-beam: a principal timber running across the shortest dimension of a building, at roof level.

Top plate: a horizontal timber at the top of the wall which supports the rafters.

Transitional house: where the traditional plan of the medieval house, parlour, hall, cross passage and service end has been abandoned with the introduction of brick chimneys. This gives rise to new plans, such as a large kitchen/ hall with a big brick chimney and a smaller unheated parlour.

Truss: timber components that define a bay, typically comprising storey posts, tie-beam and girt. An open truss lacks any studs or wall infilling. They are common where a building abuts an earlier structure.

Undershot cross-passage: where the cross passage of the open hall runs under the side of the cross-wing which projects over it. A typical feature of urban plans, representing an economical use of space.

Wall plate: topmost horizontal timber in the wall of a timber-framed building.

Wealden house: hybrid house type with a single roof covering a house plan of the cross-wing type, the side of the hall between the cross-wings being recessed under an overhanging roof.

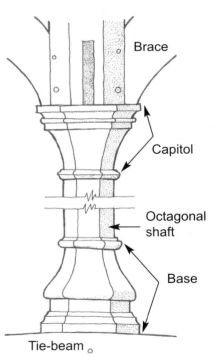

Brace

Capitol

Octagonal shaft

Base

Tie-beam

Octagonal crown post, 14 East Street

THE AUTHORS

Dave Stenning was born in Worthing, Sussex and qualified as an architect at Brighton. He worked as Conservation Officer with Colchester Borough Council and Essex County Council. He is a former President of the Essex Historic Buildings Group and a committee member of V.A.G. He is part author and illustrator of the *Essex Design Guide* and contributor to a number of articles and publications on historic buildings. He is married with two children and lives in Colchester.

Richard Shackle has been studying timber-framed buildings in North Essex since 1982. He has recorded about 300 buildings and published about 100. The buildings have been published in *Essex Archaeology and History*, The Essex Historic Buildings Group periodical and The Colchester Archaeological Group's Annual Bulletin. He specialises in creating scale drawings of buildings up to 1600.